the
Mediterranean
Table

the Mediterranean Table

Vibrant, delicious and naturally healthy
food for warm days beside the sea

RYLAND PETERS & SMALL
LONDON • NEW YORK

Senior Designer Toni Kay
Editor Miriam Catley
Production David Hearn
Art Director Leslie Harrington
Editorial Director Julia Charles
Publisher Cindy Richards
Indexer Ingrid Lock

First published in 2017 by
Ryland Peters & Small
20–21 Jockey's Fields,
London WC1R 4BW
and
341 E 116th St
New York NY 10029
www.rylandpeters.com

Recipe collection compiled by Alice Sambrook
Text © Ryland Peters & Small 2017
and contributors listed on p176
Design and photographs ©
Ryland Peters & Small 2017

ISBN: 978-1-84975-813-0

Printed and bound in China

10 9 8 7 6 5 4 3 2 1

A CIP record for this book is available from the
British Library.

US Library of Congress Cataloging-in-Publication
Data has been applied for.

NOTES

• Both British (Metric) and American (Imperial
plus US cups) measurements and ingredients are
included in these recipes for your convenience,
however it is important to work with one set of
measurements and not alternate between the
two within a recipe. Spellings are primarily British.
• All spoon measurements are level unless
otherwise specified.
• All eggs are medium (UK) or large (US), unless
specified as large, in which case US extra-large
should be used. Uncooked or partially cooked
eggs should not be served to the very old, frail,
young children, pregnant women or those with
compromised immune systems.
• When a recipe calls for the grated zest of citrus
fruit, buy unwaxed fruit and wash well before
using. If you can only find treated fruit, scrub
well in warm, soapy water and rinse before using.
• Ovens should be preheated to the specified
temperatures. We recommend using an oven
thermometer. If using a fan-assisted oven, adjust
temperatures according to the manufacturer's
instructions.
• To sterilize jars, wash them in hot, soapy water
and rinse in boiling water. Place in a large saucepan
and cover with hot water. With the saucepan lid
on, bring the water to the boil and continue boiling
for 15 minutes. Turn off the heat and leave the jars
in the hot water until just before they are to be
filled. Invert the jars onto a clean dish towel to
dry. Sterilize the lids for 5 minutes, by boiling or
according to the manufacturer's instructions. Jars
should be filled and sealed while they are still hot.

Contents

Introduction

From the sparkling shores of Santorini to the sun-dappled lemon groves of Italy this collection of recipes celebrates the very best of the Mediterranean. Packed with flavour, quick and easy to prepare and steeped in tradition, eating the Mediterranean way is not only delicious but also naturally good for you.

The first chapter, Small Bites and Plates to Share, features great ideas for summer appetizers and light snacks. There's a classic Spanish tapas board, silvery Marinated Fresh Anchovies or a gutsy Sicilian recipe for Bruschetta with Caponata and Marinated Mozzarella, all perfect accompaniments to serve with drinks.

Nothing beats a salad on a hot, sunny day, and you won't be disappointed by the recipes in the Salads and Summer Soups chapter. There's a vibrant Broad/Fava Bean, Feta and Dill Salad, striking Black Garlic Tricolore Salad and light Tomato, Melon and Feta Salad. Surprisingly refreshing soups include Gazpacho, Ajo Blanco and Tuscan Bean Soup.

Some of the very best ingredients that the Med has to offer really shine in the Sunshine Lunches chapter. For a taste of the sea try the Harissa Sardines with Tomato Salad and the Summer Tomato Tart is not only packed with Mediterranean flavours but also gloriously simple to make.

There is a long tradition of barbecuing in the Med and what better way to celebrate the summer than to fire up the grill. Recipes for a cook-up over the coals include a hearty Rack of Lamb with Harissa and Pomegranate, a decadent Grilled Lobster with simple Chive Butter and Grilled Herb-Stuffed Pork.

For entertaining on those long summer evenings the Al Fresco Feasts chapter includes a feisty, spicy Italian Polenta Puttanesca, a colourful Mediterranean Garlicky Fish Stew and Lamb Steaks with Cherry Tomatoes and Anchovy Sauce. Finally, Sweet Treats and Drinks features some of the most divine desserts and reviving drinks including an elegant Fig and Honey Ricotta Cheesecake, Sorrento Lemon Sorbet and a wickedly refreshing Limoncello.

Small bites and plates to share

From simple bowls of warm infused olives or artichokes with garlic butter to langoustines with salsa agresto and fritto misto, these divine light dishes make the perfect snack for sharing in the sunshine or work just as well served with pre-dinner drinks to kick off an al fresco meal in style.

Puttanesca relish

This relish is quite like the Olive Tapenade (see below), but it's lighter and not as rich. It can be used to add to sandwiches and recipes, but it's also lovely served with a charcuterie board and spooned onto the meats.

Pop all the ingredients into a food processor and whizz until the pieces are nice and small and the texture is relatively smooth. If you like a few small chunks, stop before it becomes more like a purée.

Transfer the mixture to a sterilized jar (see page 4) or an airtight container, or divide it between two ramekins and cover.

This relish will keep for a week or two in a sealed container in the refrigerator. It is also suitable for freezing. If you do freeze it, defrost it slowly in the refrigerator and then taste before you serve it, topping up any of the flavours that you think need a boost – perhaps the coriander/cilantro or the garlic.

Cook's Note

If you're eating this relish straightaway, you can mix in a little crème fraîche/sour cream to make it slightly creamy, if you like. This won't then keep beyond a day in the refrigerator though, so only mix it in just before you serve it.

50 g/2 oz. pitted black or Kalamata olives
2 canned anchovy fillets, drained
2 teaspoons capers, drained
a big pinch of freshly chopped coriander/cilantro
1/2 garlic clove
1 tablespoon olive oil
200-g/7-oz. can of tomatoes, drained (so you just have the pulp without too much liquid)
sea salt and freshly ground black pepper

**MAKES 1 JAR
(ABOUT 200 G/7 OZ.)**

Olive tapenade

This is a great mixture to have in a jar in the refrigerator to add to sandwiches.

50 g/2 oz. pitted black olives
2 canned anchovy fillets, drained
1 teaspoon capers, drained
1 tablespoon olive oil
a squeeze of fresh lemon juice
5 fresh basil leaves
1 teaspoon tomato purée/paste
sea salt and freshly ground black pepper

**MAKES 1 JAR
(ABOUT 200 G/7 OZ.)**

Pop all the ingredients into a food processor and whizz until the pieces are nice and small and the texture is relatively smooth.

Transfer the mixture to a sterilized jar (see page 4) or an airtight container, or divide between two ramekins and cover.

This tapenade keeps for at least a week in a sealed container in the refrigerator. It is also suitable for freezing in portions. If you do freeze it, defrost it slowly in the refrigerator and taste before you serve it – you might like to add a little more basil or a squeeze more lemon juice.

Saffron aioli

Traditional aioli is made with raw garlic, but it can become overpowering. If you like it garlicky, just add one or two cloves of crushed raw garlic instead of the roasted. It's great with fish and seafood, or try it spread on toasted sourdough and topped with fried chorizo. Healthy, no. Delicious, yes.

Preheat the oven to 220°C (425°F) Gas 7.

Drizzle a little olive oil on the garlic bulb and wrap it in kitchen foil. Roast for 30 minutes, then remove and leave to cool.

Add the saffron to the hot water and steep for 10 minutes.

Heat a pan over medium heat with a splash of oil. Add the almonds and toast until golden brown. Leave them whole or pulse them to a coarse powder, as you prefer.

In the food processor bowl or large mixing bowl, combine the egg yolk, mustard, saffron and half the water it has been steeped in. Start blending/whisking, pouring in the vegetable oil in a slow and steady stream, mixing all the time. Don't add it too fast or you'll end up with a curdled mixture. It should emulsify with the egg yolk to make a thick paste. Next, slowly add the olive oil. If it looks too thick, add a splash of saffron water. Once all the oil has been added, add the roasted garlic (give the foil a few pricks and squeeze; it should come out easily). Add the lemon juice and toasted almonds, then season boldly.

150 ml/²/₃ cup olive oil
1 whole head garlic
1 tablespoon hot water
a small pinch (about ¹/₄ teaspoon) saffron threads
30 g/¹/₃ cup flaked/sliced almonds
2 egg yolks
1 teaspoon Dijon mustard
150 ml/²/₃ cup vegetable oil
freshly squeezed juice of ¹/₂ lemon
sea salt and freshly ground black pepper

FILLS A 455 G/1 LB. JAR

Hazelnut picada

A delicious, crunchy mixture that can be sprinkled on virtually anything. It goes particularly well with grilled/broiled pork. Be sure to add it at the last minute or it will soak up any liquids in the vicinity and go soggy. Once prepared it should last for a good week or so in an airtight container.

Heat a non-stick frying pan/skillet over medium heat. Add the olive oil and bread, along with the garlic. Fry the bread on both sides until deeply golden. Remove the bread with a fish slice/slotted turner, sprinkle with salt and leave to drain on kitchen paper/paper towel. Discard the fried garlic from the pan (it was only in there to flavour the oil) and add the hazelnuts, rosemary and chilli/chile. Fry until the hazelnuts have turned golden, then remove from the heat.

Roughly chop the fried bread and add to the hazelnuts, along with the orange zest and chopped mint. Stir well and season with salt to taste.

100 ml/¹/₃ cup olive oil
2 slices rustic white bread (ideally sourdough)
4 garlic cloves, bashed
100 g/³/₄ cup shelled skinned hazelnuts
1 sprig fresh rosemary, chopped
1 red chilli/chile (optional), finely chopped
grated zest of ¹/₂ orange
1 sprig fresh mint, chopped
sea salt

FILLS A 455 G/1 LB. JAR

Italian bean dip

All around the Mediterranean, fresh and dried peas, beans and lentils are used in dips and spreads, as sauces with pasta and in soups. The best are skinless dried broad beans, known as fava, or faba beans. Soak them for 4 hours or overnight in cold water, or cheat by putting them in a saucepan, covering them with boiling water, bringing them to the boil and soaking for 2 hours with the heat turned off. Drain, cover with cold water, bring to the boil and simmer until tender. Drain again, season and use as a dip or spread.

Soak and drain the beans as described above, then put them in a large saucepan with the bunch of herbs, onion and potato and add 2 litres boiling water. Bring to the boil, boil hard for 10 minutes, reduce the heat and cook, part-covered for 1½–2 hours or until you can crush the beans easily with your thumbnail.

Drain the vegetables, reserving 2–3 tablespoons of liquid. Discard the herbs.

Working in batches if necessary, put the beans, potato, onion and raw garlic in a food processor, with the olive oil, lemon juice, oregano, salt and pepper. Blend in short bursts to a grainy but creamy purée.

Serve hot (as a side dish), warm or cool, sprinkled with extra olive oil. Serve as a dip or spread with baby leafy vegetables, radishes and cucumber or with bread.

400 g/2 cups dried skinned fava beans

1 fresh bouquet garni of parsley, celery, bay leaf and thyme

1 large onion, coarsely chopped

1 potato, unpeeled

4 garlic cloves, chopped

60 ml/¼ cup good-quality extra virgin olive oil, plus extra to serve (optional)

freshly squeezed juice of 1 lemon (4–5 tablespoons)

6 sprigs of fresh oregano, chopped

sea salt and freshly ground black pepper, to serve

YOUR CHOICE OF:

baby leafy vegetables

radishes

crusty bread

cucumber

SERVES 4

Spanish clams with ham

Mediterranean live clams usually go straight into the cooking pot, with oil and garlic. Herbs and a splash of wine are sometimes added. However, because Spanish cured hams are so exceptional, adding even a little will season and enliven many such savoury dishes. Mar i montaña (sea and mountains) is a typically Catalan cooking idea which has spread worldwide. Catalans also revel in extraordinary seasonings, aromatic herbs, chocolate, juniper, cinnamon with game and saffron in both sweet and savoury dishes. A revelation.

2 tablespoons extra virgin olive oil

500 g/1 lb. live clams in the shell, or frozen raw clams

50 g/2 oz. jamón serrano or Parma ham, cut into thin strips

1 small green chilli/chile, deseeded and chopped

2 garlic cloves, sliced

4 tablespoons white wine or cider

2 tablespoons chopped spring onion/ scallion tops, chives or parsley

SERVES 4

Put the olive oil, clams, ham, chilli/chile and garlic in a flameproof casserole and stir over high heat. When the ham is cooked and the clams begin to open, add the wine, cover the pan and tilt it several times to mix the ingredients. Cook on high for a further 2–3 minutes or until all the clams have opened and are cooked.

Sprinkle with chopped spring onions/ scallions. Cover again for 1 minute, then ladle into shallow soup bowls.

Greek cheese savoury

Although often served towards the end of a Greek meal (like an old-fashioned cheese savoury used to be), this dish may also be served as a starter, part of a meze (literally, a 'tableful'). Unlike the Cypriot version, which uses local haloumi cheese, the traditional saganaki uses strongly flavoured, hard, dry, seasonal cheese such as kefalotyri. If unavailable, use mature Cheddar instead. Traditionally this is served in small, two-handled frying pans brought, sizzling, to the table. The cheese is eaten with a fork or scooped onto crusty bread. Use best-quality olive oil: its taste makes a considerable difference.

4 slices kefalotyri cheese or mature Cheddar, cut 5 mm/¹⁄₄ in. thick
plain/all-purpose flour, for dusting
good-quality extra virgin olive oil, for cooking (preferably Greek)
coarsely ground black pepper
lemon wedges, to serve

SERVES 4

Dust each slice of cheese generously with flour, patting it all over. Heat 2 teaspoons of olive oil for each cheese piece (cook them singly or in pairs, depending on the size of the pan) in a small frying pan/skillet until very hot. Using tongs, add 1–2 slices of floured cheese. Fry for 1–1¹⁄₂ minutes or until golden, crusty and aromatic and starting to soften inside.

Using a narrow spatula, carefully turn each piece over. Fry for a further 45 seconds on the second side until crusty.

Serve directly from the dish, adding black pepper and a wedge of lemon, or slide onto a small plate. Continue until all the cheese is cooked. Eat while still hot, crusty, fragrant and starting to melt.

Chorizo in red wine

Chorizo, a paprika-rich, spicy, smoky, garlicky and sometimes piquant Spanish sausage, can be bought in links or in long, curved shapes, raw or cooked. It varies, depending on its area of production and the uses for which it is intended. Some types, larger and sold cooked and ready-sliced like salami, are also available as snack foods. This recipe needs the raw, spicy, link-type chorizo meant for cooking. Find it in good specialist delicatessens or Hispanic grocers.

Cut the chorizo into 1-cm/½-in. chunks. Heat half the oil in a large, non-stick frying pan/skillet until very hot. Add half the chorizo and fry on both sides for 1 minute each. Remove with a slotted spoon and keep hot. Add the remaining oil and remaining chorizo. Cook and remove as before.

Add the wine and thyme, if using, to the pan and swirl to dissolve the sediment. Cook gently to thicken and reduce the sauce. Pour the sauce over the hot chorizo, sprinkle with pepper and serve with chunks of torn bread for dipping.

750 g/1½ lb. uncooked chorizo sausage, or other dense, garlic-flavoured pork sausage

2 tablespoons extra virgin olive oil

150 ml/⅔ cup red Rioja wine

4 sprigs of fresh thyme (optional)

freshly ground black pepper

torn bread, for dipping

SERVES 4

Artichoke with garlic butter

Stunning to look at and simple to cook, an artichoke often scares cooks due to its rugged appearance and often complicated methods to cook and prepare. Try this simple recipe and serve with garlic butter as finger food.

4 globe artichokes
200 g/1³/4 sticks salted butter
2 garlic cloves, crushed
50 g/²/3 cup grated Parmesan cheese
freshly ground black pepper, to season

SERVES 4

Trim the base of each artichoke so it can stand upright. Slice across the artichoke top, about 3 cm/1¼ in. from the top, to display the inner leaf patterns.

Transfer the artichokes to a large covered pan of salted water and simmer over a low heat for 30 minutes.

Heat the butter in a small pan until it just begins to foam. Add the crushed garlic to the foaming butter and remove from the heat; stir a couple of times to distribute the garlic and set aside.

Place the steaming hot artichokes in four serving bowls. Drizzle with the garlic butter and top with Parmesan. Finish with a sprinkle of black pepper and serve.

To eat the artichoke, pluck each petal and squeeze the petal between your teeth pulling out the fleshy centre from the base. When all the petals have been eaten, remove the furry choke with a teaspoon then eat the core of the artichoke, mopping up the remaining butter and cheese. This is messy eating at its delicious best!

Warm infused olives

These olives are perfect to serve with any cured meats. Make sure you put some crusty bread with them too, so that guests can soak up the delicious oil.

Start with about one-third of the olive oil in a frying pan/skillet, heat it over medium heat, then add the garlic, chilli/chile, ginger and lime juice, and fry until the garlic and chilli/chile pieces are brown and crispy. Add the rest of the olive oil and continue to fry until bubbling.

Reduce the heat right down to a simmer and throw in the olives. Stir for a few minutes to heat them through, making sure that the olives don't cook on the bottom of the frying pan/skillet.

Remove from the heat, add salt and pepper to taste, then transfer the mixture to a heatproof dish. Serve.

This mixture will keep in the refrigerator for up to 5 days; you might just have to warm it through again before serving to melt any oil that has set.

3 tablespoons olive oil
1 garlic clove, finely chopped
¹/4 fresh red chilli/chile, deseeded and finely chopped
a pinch of ground ginger
a good squeeze of fresh lime juice
150–200 g/5–7 oz. unseasoned green wor black olives
sea salt and freshly ground black pepper

SERVES 2

4 tablespoons olive oil

2 garlic cloves, chopped

2 small dried red chillies/chiles, crumbled

450 g/1 lb. raw prawns/shrimp, peeled, deveined, rinsed and dried

1 teaspoon sweet smoked Spanish paprika

1 tablespoon finely chopped fresh parsley

sea salt

crusty bread, to serve

SERVES 4 AS A TAPAS DISH

Heat the olive oil in a heavy-based frying pan/skillet. Add the chopped garlic and fry briefly, stirring, until fragrant. Add the crumbled chillies/chiles, mixing well, then add the prawns/shrimp, mixing to coat them in the oil.

Fry the prawns/shrimp briefly, stirring, until they turn opaque and pink on both sides, taking care not to over-cook them and dry them out. Season with salt, then add the Spanish paprika, mixing in. Sprinkle with parsley and serve at once with crusty bread.

Spanish garlic prawns/shrimp

This quick-to-cook classic tapas dish, made from a few simple ingredients including garlic and smoked Spanish paprika, is addictively moreish. Cook and serve it at once as a first course or as part of a tapas feast. Do make sure you have plenty of bread on hand for soaking up the flavourful olive oil.

Patatas bravas

Fried potatoes in a spicy tomato sauce is a popular and traditional Spanish tapas dish. Serve with good-quality cured ham, such as jamón serrano or Parma ham/prosciutto, and a glass of chilled fino Sherry as an appetizing first course.

Boil the potatoes in salted boiling water until just tender; drain, cool and dice.

Meanwhile, prepare the spicy tomato sauce. Heat 1 tablespoon of the oil in a small, heavy-bottomed frying pan/skillet. Add the shallot and garlic and crumble in the dried chilli/chile. Fry, stirring, for 1–2 minutes until fragrant.

Add the Sherry vinegar and continue to cook for 1 minute, until syrupy. Add the canned tomatoes and mix well. Season with salt, pepper and the smoked paprika/pimentón. Turn up the heat and bring to the boil. Cook the sauce uncovered, stirring often to break down the tomatoes, for 10–15 minutes, until reduced and thickened.

In a separate large frying pan/skillet, heat the remaining olive oil. Add the cooled, diced potatoes and fry until golden brown on all sides, stirring often and seasoning with salt. Pour the cooked tomato sauce over the potatoes, garnish with parsley and serve hot or at room temperature.

300 g/10 oz. waxy potatoes, peeled
2 tablespoons olive oil
1 shallot, chopped
1 garlic clove, chopped
1 dried chilli/chile
1 tablespoon sherry vinegar
400 g/14 oz. canned plum tomatoes
sea salt and freshly ground black pepper
1 teaspoon hot smoked paprika/pimentón
freshly chopped parsley, to garnish

SERVES 4

Grilled wild garlic/ramps mussels

A rich, tasty way to serve mussels, this offers a great contrast of textures between the crunchy crumb crust and the juicy mussel flesh below.

Rinse the mussels well under cold running water, discarding any that are open or cracked. Scrub well to remove any beards or grit.

Put the cleaned mussels in a large pan, adding cold water to a depth of 2.5 cm/1 in. up the side of the pan. Set the pan over a medium heat, cover and cook the mussels for around 5 minutes, until they have steamed open.

Drain the mussels, discarding any that haven't opened during the cooking process.

Once the mussels are cool enough to handle, pull one half of each shell off each mussel, leaving the mussel anchored in the remaining half. Place the mussels, shell-side-down, on a baking sheet.

Mix together the breadcrumbs, wild garlic/ramps and olive oil, seasoning with salt and freshly ground pepper. Spoon a little of the breadcrumb mixture over each mussel, so that it forms a topping.

Preheat a grill/broiler to its highest setting and cook the topped mussels for 2–3 minutes until the crumb topping turns golden brown. Serve at once.

1 kg/2¼ lbs. mussels
30 g/⅓ cup fresh breadcrumbs
15 g/¼ cup wild garlic leaves/ramps, thoroughly rinsed and very finely chopped
60 ml/¼ cup extra virgin olive oil
sea salt and freshly ground black pepper

SERVES 4 AS A STARTER/APPETIZER OR 2 AS A MAIN/ENTRÉE

200 g/1²/₃ cups plain/all-purpose flour

1 egg plus 1 egg yolk

200 ml/³/₄ cup milk

sea salt and freshly ground black pepper

150 g/5 oz. whitebait/smelt
   (or micro-fry whitebait)

15 g/1 tablespoon butter

vegetable oil, for frying

mayonnaise, to serve

¹/₂ lemon, cut into wedges to serve

SERVES 2

Whitebait fritters

Whitebait are a delicacy and a delight if treated with respect when cooked. 'Whitebait' refers to the micro-fry of several small species of fish, herrings and sprats being the more common types. In the United Kingdom, whitebait are larger but still served whole so the recipe here is not a true fritter, but just as delicious.

Sift the flour into a large mixing bowl and add the egg and egg yolk. Stir well, then slowly add all of the milk, stirring as you do – you should end up with a thick batter. Add a generous pinch of salt and black pepper and mix through. Now add the whitebait and carefully fold them through the mixture.

Put the butter and enough vegetable oil to just cover the base in a frying pan/skillet and set over a medium heat until the butter is foaming.

If the whitebait are larger than micro-fry (as pictured), carefully place the battered whitebait in the pan and cook for 3–4 minutes until golden brown, turning once. If you are using micro-fry, using a serving spoon, scoop a portion of the whitebait batter mixture into the pan. Cook for 2–3 minutes till golden brown on one side then flip the whitebait and cook on the other side until brown and cooked through.

Remove the cooked whitebait or fritters from the pan using a slotted spoon and drain on paper towels to absorb any excess oil, then serve immediately with mayonnaise and lemon wedges for squeezing, or keep warm in a low oven for up to 30 minutes.

Tempura squid

Tempura is a lighter form of battered squid. It's light and delicious and almost too easy to make. A great alternative to fish and chips, try it served with some raw vegetables on a hot day.

2 medium squid
vegetable oil, for frying
100 g/³⁄₄ cup plain/all-purpose flour
50 g/¹⁄₂ cup cornflour/cornstarch
10 g/1 tablespoon baking powder
100 ml/¹⁄₃ cup chilled sparkling water
sea salt and freshly ground black pepper
sweet chilli/chile sauce or aioli, to serve

a deep-fat fryer

SERVES 2–4

Begin by preparing the squid following the instructions below, then cut the body into bite-sized portions.

Preheat a deep-fat fryer to 180°C (350°F) or fill a deep saucepan with oil and set over a medium heat to warm through.

Make the batter by stirring together the flour, cornflour/cornstarch and baking powder to a thick paste with a little sparkling water in a large mixing bowl. When ready to cook add the remaining chilled sparkling water to make a thin paste. Add the squid pieces to the batter then carefully place in the hot oil in the fryer and cook for 2 minutes. Remove the squid from the fryer and drain on paper towels for a few seconds, sprinkle with a little salt and pepper and serve immediately with a dip of either sweet chilli/chile sauce or aioli.

Tip
Drop a little batter into the oil to test if it is hot enough. It should fizz and cook in 20 seconds. It will brown if the oil is too hot and stay soft if too cool.

How to prepare squid
1 Gently pull the head away from the body taking the milky white intestines with it and cut off the tentacles from the head.

2 Squeeze out the beak-like mouth from the centre of the tentacles, cut away and discard.

3 Reach into the body and pull out the plastic-like quill and any soft white roe.

4 Scrape the outside of the head clean, removing any skin.

5 Pull off the two fins from either side of the body, slice the head open and wash the pouch with water.

Langoustines with salsa agresto

Langoustines, the ones that look like mini lobsters, have the most delicious sweet and delicate flesh, perfect for a summer BBQ or if the weather is against you, on a pan inside. Here they are served very simply with the Italian salsa agresto, which is not a million miles away from a pesto sauce.

65 g/½ cup fresh walnuts, plus a few extra to serve, chopped into chunks

35 g/¼ cup almonds

1 small garlic clove

a small handful fresh flat-leaf parsley, leaves only

15–20 fresh basil leaves

extra virgin olive oil

½ lemon, zested and 2 teaspoons freshly squeezed juice

sea salt and freshly ground black pepper

12 langoustines

SERVES 4

Preheat the oven to 180°C (350°F) Gas 4.

For the salsa agresto, place the walnuts and almonds on separate baking sheets in the oven for about 5 minutes, until a shade darker and aromatic. Leave to cool and rub the walnuts to remove any loose skin.

Put the walnuts into a food processor with the almonds, garlic and herbs and blitz until you almost have a smooth paste, scraping down the sides every now and then. While blitzing, slowly pour in 100 ml/scant ½ cup of olive oil and the lemon juice and zest. Season with ¼ teaspoon salt and some pepper. Taste and adjust if necessary.

Lay the langoustines on their backs and cut in half lengthways down the centre. Lightly oil the langoustines and season with a little salt and pepper. Heat a frying pan/skillet over a medium–high heat and place them flesh-side down on the pan/skillet. Cook for 2 minutes then flip over and cook for about 30 seconds.

Tangle 6 langoustine halves onto each plate, drizzle over the salsa agresto and scatter some of the chopped walnuts on top. Serve immediately.

Spanish board

Spanish tapas is the tradition of serving little dishes of food with drinks. Traditional tapas include hams and chorizo, but they are also accompanied by some wonderful non-meat dishes. There is a huge variety of options, from hot to cold.

SUGGESTED ACCOMPANIMENTS:

Patatas Bravas (see page 21)

Olives

Marinated roasted red peppers

Rustic Spanish breads

Manchego cheese

Almonds

The best-known Spanish cured meat is, without doubt, chorizo. This is made from minced/ground and seasoned pork, which gains its a lovely smoky flavour from paprika and chilli/chile. The mix is stuffed into a casing and hung to air-dry. It can be eaten as it is and is also very adaptable for cooked recipes – perhaps more so than salami, because it contains slightly more oil.

Jamón Serrano (literally 'ham from the mountains') is whole cured ham, similar to prosciutto, and is usually served in thin slices. It has a lovely rich, dark flavour and comes from regions all over Spain.

Jamón Ibérico is a protected origin variety of Spanish cured ham (pictured opposite). Jamón Ibérico de Bellota is one of the most expensive meat products in the world. The pigs – usually Landrace breed – traditionally live to 2 years old and roam free in forests. For the last few months of their lives, they gorge happily on acorns, which adds around 20% more fat to them. The meat is so oily and fatty that when the hind leg is hung to air-dry, a little vessel is hung below to capture the oil that drips. It's rich, delicious and expensive. Chorizo Ibérico de Bellota is also popular and pricey; made from the comminuted shoulder and neck meat from those acorn-guzzling Iberian pigs.

Cecina de León is a hind-leg of cured beef from the León region of Spain. The Spanish Cecina meat range occasionally uses horse- and goatmeat as well, however it is always produced by a dry salt-cure and hanging process. When sliced, it is a vibrant shade of maroon, with darker brown at the edges.

What to pair with your platter:
You could opt for a classic red such as Rioja, Tempranillo or Garnarcha, or really inspire that holiday mood with a refreshing, cold Spanish beer. A Spanish platter works very well with a fino sherry — it may not be the first thing you think of when selecting wines to serve with a platter of cured meats, but a dry sherry is a perfect pairing with Spanish meats. A dry rosé, such as one from the Navarra, would complement the rich flavours of the meats too.

A chilled glass of Cava is a good choice with the strong paprika-based flavours of chorizo.

Parma ham and melon

This is such a classic appetizer and what it lacks in imagination and flair, it gains in everyone still having plenty of room for a lovely big main course/entrée. So don't knock it until you've had seconds of dessert, when you'll thank it.

8 slices Parma ham/prosciutto
¹/₂ melon, peeled, deseeded and sliced into thin slices
4 squeezes of fresh lime juice
4 pinches of freshly ground black pepper

SERVES 4

Divide the ham and melon evenly between the serving plates. Either place the Parma ham/prosciutto and melon neatly on the plate next to each other or wrap the Parma ham around the slices of melon. Squeeze lime juice over the top of each serving and sprinkle with pepper.

Fried vegetables with tomato sauce

Fritto misto, or mixed fried food, is an Italian staple, found mainly in Sicily. Fritto misto consists of small morsels of vegetables, such as aubergine/eggplant and asparagus, in batter or breadcrumbs, which are deep fried and eaten straight away. Courgette/zucchini flowers also work well when battered and deep fried. The inclusion of chilli/chile and cloves in the tomato sauce reveals an Arab influence on this dish.

olive oil, for deep frying

Italian '00' flour, for dusting

1 kg/2¹/₄ lbs. mixed vegetables, e.g. (bell) peppers, aubergine/eggplant, asparagus, courgettes/zucchini, cut into 5-cm/2-in. strips

TOMATO SAUCE

2 tablespoons olive oil

2 shallots, finely chopped

2 garlic cloves, finely chopped

500 g/3 cups ripe tomatoes, chopped

3 teaspoons crushed dried chilli/chile (pepperoncino)

2 cloves

sea salt and freshly ground black pepper

tomato purée/paste, to taste (optional)

a handful of flat-leaf parsley, finely chopped (optional)

BATTER

300 ml/1¹/₄ cups milk

1 yolk

¹/₂ teaspoon sea salt

125 g/1 scant cup Italian '00' flour

¹/₂ teaspoon baking powder

SERVES 4–6

To make the sauce, heat the oil in a medium-sized saucepan and cook the shallots for about 4 minutes over medium heat, until golden. Add the garlic and cook until soft. Add the tomato, chilli/chile, cloves and salt and pepper.

Simmer gently for 20 minutes until thick and pulpy. Set aside, picking out the cloves (if you want to increase the colour to be a more vibrant red, add a little tomato purée/paste and continue cooking for 12 more minutes).

To make the batter, whisk together the milk, egg yolk and salt in a large bowl for about 3 minutes, or until smooth. Sift the flour into the bowl with the baking powder, and whisk together.

Heat 4 cm/1¹/₂ in. of olive oil in a deep frying pan/skillet. Spread a little flour on a plate. Dip the vegetable pieces one at a time into the flour and then in the batter to coat. Carefully drop into the oil in batches and cook for about 2 minutes, until golden. Drain well on paper towels.

Stir the parsley into the sauce, if using, and serve alongside the warm fritto misto.

Sicilian potato croquettes

The Sicilian dialect word 'cazzilli' was jestingly given to these crispy croquettes on account of their shape. Friggitoria (fry shops) all over Palermo sell this super finger food in many different guises.

Place the potatoes in a medium-sized saucepan of boiling water. Keep the potatoes cooking but not boiling (boiling will encourage the skins to burst). Cook for about 15 minutes, or until tender.

When the potatoes are tender, drain and leave to cool. Peel away the skins and press the potatoes through a ricer or food mill into a bowl. Don't use a food processor as this will develop the starch too much.

Add the salt, pepper, nutmeg, butter and parsley. Mix well and form into 10 x 7.5-cm/4 x 3-in. pieces. Roll into smaller rods (fork-friendly, size-wise).

Dip the rods into the beaten egg and then the breadcrumbs. Place on a parchment-lined tray and chill in the refrigerator for 30 minutes.

Heat the oil and fry in batches until golden. Drain on paper towels. Serve hot.

4 medium-sized (all the same size is preferable) old potatoes (i.e. King Edward, Desiree, Pentland Crown, Maris Piper, Rooster), cleaned

$^1/_2$ teaspoon ground nutmeg

75 g/5 tablespoons unsalted butter

a generous handful of flat-leaf parsley, freshly chopped

2 UK large/US extra large eggs, beaten

150 g/1$^1/_4$ cups dried breadcrumbs

olive oil or groundnut oil, for deep frying

sea salt and freshly ground black pepper

SERVES 4–6

Fried courgette/zucchini flowers

Some market stalls and vegetable shops will sell the delicate courgette/ zucchini flowers when they're in season but the best come from your very own plot. Be sure to keep them fresh in iced water before you cook them as they deteriorate very quickly.

7 g/1$^1/_4$ teaspoons fresh yeast (or 1 teaspoon dried/active dry yeast)

450 ml/1$^3/_4$ cups warm water (37°C/99°F)

250 g/2 cups Italian '00' flour, sifted

2 tablespoons olive oil

groundnut/peanut oil, for frying

24 large courgette/zucchini flowers

a handful of flat-leaf parsley, freshly chopped

lemon quarters, to serve

sea salt and freshly ground black pepper

SERVES 4–6

Dissolve the fresh yeast in a little of the water and set aside for 10 minutes. If using dried yeast, mix with the flour.

Mix the flour, water, oil, yeast mixture and salt and pepper well, using a whisk to beat out any lumps. Cover and leave to become bubbly for 45–60 minutes. Stir the bubbles in the batter.

Heat 8 cm/3 in. of groundnut/peanut oil in a deep pan. Remove the stamens from the courgette/zucchini flowers. Dip the flowers one at a time into the batter and shake off the excess.

Place one at a time in the oil, frying 4 at a time until golden, turning once. Remove with a slotted spoon and drain on paper towels, then sprinkle with parsley and salt. Serve straight away with lemon quarters.

Arancini with pecorino, porcini & mozzarella

You can use leftover risotto for these rice balls if you happen to have any, but as they are so delicious it's worth making the risotto especially. They can be prepared and rolled in advance; coat them and fry just before serving.

Soak the porcini in a small bowl of boiling water for about 15 minutes, or until soft. Drain well on paper towels and finely chop.

Heat the olive oil and butter in a medium saucepan and add the shallots, garlic and chopped porcini. Cook over low–medium heat until soft but not coloured. Add the rice to the pan and stir to coat well in the buttery mixture. Gradually add the vegetable stock – add it one ladleful at a time, and as the stock is absorbed by the rice, add another ladleful, stirring as you do so. Continue cooking in this way until the rice is al dente and the stock is used up. Remove the pan from the heat, add the pecorino and herbs and season well with salt and black pepper. Tip the risotto into a bowl and leave to cool completely.

Once the rice is cold, divide it into walnut-sized pieces and roll into balls. Taking one ball at a time, flatten it into a disc in the palm of your hand, press some diced mozzarella in the middle and wrap the rice around it to completely encase the cheese. Shape into a neat ball. Repeat with the remaining risotto.

Tip the flour, beaten eggs and breadcrumbs into separate shallow bowls. Roll the rice balls first in the flour, then coat well in the eggs and finally, roll them in the breadcrumbs to completely coat.

Fill a deep-fat fryer with sunflower oil or pour oil to a depth of about 5 cm/2 in. into a deep saucepan. Heat until a cube of bread sizzles and browns in about 5 seconds. Cook the arancini, in batches, in the hot oil for 3–4 minutes or until crisp, hot and golden brown. Drain on paper towels and serve.

15 g/¹/₂ oz. dried porcini mushrooms

1 tablespoon olive oil

30 g/2 tablespoons unsalted butter

2 shallots, finely chopped

1 fat garlic clove, crushed

250 g/1¹/₄ cups risotto rice (arborio or carnaroli)

750–850 ml/3–3¹/₂ cups hot vegetable stock

40 g/¹/₃ cup freshly grated pecorino cheese

1 tablespoon freshly chopped flat-leaf parsley or oregano

125 g/4 oz. mozzarella cheese, diced

100 g/³/₄ cup plain/all-purpose flour

2 eggs, lightly beaten

200 g/2 cups fresh, fine breadcrumbs

about 1 litre/4 cups sunflower oil, for frying

sea salt and freshly ground black pepper

a deep-fat fryer

MAKES 15–18

Three marinated antipasti

All too often, antipasti can be very dull, but with a little imagination, you can work wonders with the simplest of ingredients. Marinating these morsels first gives them extra flavour. The best antipasti are an appealing mix of colours, flavours and textures, to whet the palate before the meal ahead.

INVOLTINI DI PEPERONI

2 large red (bell) peppers

150 g/6 oz. mozzarella cheese

8 large fresh basil leaves

1 tablespoon Classic Pesto (page 137)

extra virgin olive oil

sea salt and freshly ground black pepper

MELANZANE CON SALAME E CARCIOFI

1 medium aubergine/eggplant, about 200 g/8 oz.

6 tablespoons olive oil, plus extra for brushing

8 thin slices salami

4 artichokes marinated in oil, drained and halved

2 tablespoons freshly squeezed lemon juice

1 tablespoon capers, rinsed, drained and chopped

sea salt and freshly ground black pepper

ZUCCHINE ALLA GRIGLIA MARINATE AL LIMONE

3 medium courgettes/zucchini

4 tablespoons olive oil, plus extra for brushing

2 tablespoons freshly squeezed lemon juice

1 tablespoon freshly grated Parmesan cheese

2 anchovies, rinsed and finely chopped

cocktail sticks/toothpicks

SERVES 4

To make the involtini, chargrill the (bell) peppers until soft and black. Rinse off the charred skin, cut the peppers in quarters lengthways, cut off the stalks and scrape out the seeds. Cut the mozzarella into 8 thin slices. Put a slice inside each pepper strip, put a basil leaf on top and season well with salt and pepper. Roll up from one end and secure with a cocktail stick/toothpick. Put the pesto in a bowl and beat in enough olive oil to thin it to pouring consistency. Add the rolls and toss to coat. Cover and let marinate for at least 2 hours.

To make the melanzane, heat a ridged stove-top grill pan until hot. Cut the aubergine/eggplant into 8 thin slices, brush lightly with olive oil and cook for 2–3 minutes on each side. Put a slice of salami on each one, then a halved artichoke at one side. Fold the aubergine/eggplant in half to cover the artichoke, secure with a cocktail stick/toothpick and put in a shallow dish. Put the 6 tablespoons olive oil in a bowl, whisk in the lemon juice, capers, salt and pepper, then spoon over the aubergines/eggplants. Cover and let marinate as above.

To make the zucchine, cut the courgettes/zucchini into long thin slices, brush with olive oil and cook on the same grill pan for 2–3 minutes on each side. Transfer to a shallow dish. Put the 4 tablespoons olive oil, lemon juice, Parmesan and anchovies in a bowl, beat with a fork, then pour over the courgettes/zucchini. Cover and leave to marinate as above. Serve all three as mixed antipasti.

Marinated fresh anchovies

There's nothing quite like these light, fresh, silvery morsels eaten fillet by fillet with a glass of chilled vino bianco, overlooking a peacock sea, with a warm salty breeze on your face. They are mild and fresh, and the combination of lemon, parsley and olive oil is lifted by the zing of spring onion/scallions. Anchovies are easy to find, but you can make this dish with any small fish.

To clean the anchovies, cut off the heads and slit open the bellies. Remove the insides (there isn't very much there at all) under running water. Slide your thumb along the backbone to release the flesh along its length. Take hold of the backbone at the head end and lift it out. The fish should now open up like a book. At this stage you can decide whether to cut it into 2 long fillets or leave whole – size will dictate. Pat them dry with paper towels.

Pour the lemon juice through a strainer into a shallow non-reactive dish and add the anchovies in an even layer, skin side up. Cover and leave to marinate in the refrigerator for 24 hours.

The next day, lift them out of the lemon juice – they will look pale and 'cooked'. Arrange them on a serving dish. Sprinkle with the spring onion/scallions, parsley and a large quantity of olive oil, season with salt and pepper and serve at room temperature.

16 fresh anchovies, small sardines or sprats

freshly squeezed juice of 2 lemons

2 spring onions/scallions, thinly sliced

2 tablespoons freshly chopped flat-leaf parsley

extra virgin olive oil

sea salt and freshly ground black pepper

SERVES 4

Sardine crostini

These crostini can make a lovely light lunch or you can scale down the recipe to make canapés. Salty, grilled sardines work perfectly with the flavour of fresh tomatoes.

Toast the bread slices under a medium grill/broiler until lightly golden.

Rub the garlic cut-side down on each slice of toasted bread. This will give a hint of garlic to the finished crostinis but it won't overpower the other flavours in the dish.

Preheat a frying pan/skillet over a medium heat. Add the sardines to the dry pan to cook for about 10 minutes, turning the fish every minute or so, until they are cooked through and slightly blackened.

Take the pan off the heat and immediately add the onions. After 30 seconds add the tomatoes. There should be enough residual heat in the pan to heat the tomatoes through but not overcook them.

Place 2 sardines on each slice of toasted bread, cover with a few spoonfuls of tomato and onion mixture. Dress with a few basil leaves and season with salt and pepper before serving.

4 slices crusty white bread

1 garlic clove, cut in half

8 whole sardines (each about 100 g/ 3^{1}/$_{2}$ oz.), scaled, gutted and heads and tails discarded

2 brown onions, sliced into rings

4 tomatoes, diced into 5-mm/^{1}/$_{4}$-in. pieces

a small bunch of fresh basil, to serve

sea salt and freshly ground black pepper, to season

MAKES 4

Bruschetta of caponata and marinated mozzarella

Caponata is one of the gutsiest most robust Sicilian dishes. An old favourite, it can go round for round with the meatiest of stews. It keeps well, so it's worth making an extra-large batch. It generally tastes best when served at room temperature. The marinated mozzarella is a dish unto itself, and a cheat's way of making ordinary mozzarella taste like creamy burrata. Scattered with some cherry tomatoes and a little homemade pesto, it becomes a perfect summer appetizer. In this recipe, the soft unctuousness balances perfectly with the in-your-face caponata.

For the marinated mozzarella, rip the mozzarella into rough chunks. Combine with the other ingredients and allow to marinate for 30 minutes.

Meanwhile, for the caponata, take a deep saucepan and pour in enough

vegetable oil to come one third of the way up the pan. Heat the oil to 180°C (350°F), or until an aubergine/eggplant cube sizzles nicely without the oil bubbling too aggressively. Fry the aubergine/eggplant in batches until deep golden. Remove and allow to drain on paper towels.

Heat the olive oil in a heavy-based pan or casserole dish. Add the garlic and fry until browned, then remove and set aside. Add the onion, celery, (bell) peppers, olives and capers. Fry until the onion is translucent and beginning to caramelize – about 10 minutes. Add the pine nuts and raisins and fry for 2 minutes. Add the tomato passata and stir to incorporate everything. Put the vinegar and sugar in a cup and stir to dissolve the sugar. Add to the pan and cook for 15 minutes, stirring. Season to taste, but don't wimp out, as it needs a bold amount of salt. Remove from the heat and allow to cool slightly before adding the basil.

Toast the bread, rub each slice twice with the halved garlic and layer some basil leaves over it (this helps stop the toast getting soggy). Spoon the caponata and marinated mozzarella over the top and serve.

2 thick slices sourdough bread

1 garlic clove, halved

sea salt and freshly ground black pepper

MARINATED MOZZARELLA

125 g/4¹/2 oz. mozzarella cheese balls

2 tablespoons crème fraîche/soured cream

1 tablespoon double/heavy cream

1 tablespoon olive oil

grated zest of ¹/2 lemon

5 large, fresh basil leaves, finely chopped, plus extra whole leaves, to serve

CAPONATA

vegetable oil, for frying

2 large aubergines/eggplants, cubed

3 tablespoons olive oil

3 garlic cloves, bashed

1 red onion, finely chopped

2 celery sticks, finely sliced

1 red (bell) pepper, cut into strips

1 yellow (bell) pepper, cut into strips

60 g/¹/2 cup large green olives, bashed to help remove the stone/pit, then torn into chunks

40 g/4 tablespoons capers

50 g/¹/3 cup pine nuts

25 g/2 tablespoons raisins

150 ml/²/3 cup tomato passata (or a good-quality jarred tomato sauce)

5 tablespoons red wine vinegar

1 tablespoon sugar

a bunch of fresh basil, roughly chopped

SERVES 2 AS A STARTER/ APPETIZER

Cherry tomato bruschetta

Juicy tomatoes contrast nicely with the crunchiness of the baked bread in this vibrant, classic Italian snack. Serve as a rustic start to a meal, a midday snack or lunchtime treat.

Preheat the oven to 200°C (400°F) Gas 6.

Slice the baguette into 1-cm½-in. thick slices. Transfer to a baking sheet and lightly brush with 1 teaspoon of the olive oil. Bake in the preheated oven for 20 minutes, until pale gold and crisp. Remove from the oven and set aside to cool.

Meanwhile, mix together the cherry tomato quarters with the remaining olive oil, balsamic vinegar, salt and whole garlic clove in a large bowl. Shred the basil leaves and mix in. Set aside to allow the flavours to infuse while the baguette slices bake and cool.

Discard the garlic clove from the tomato mixture, then spoon onto each slice of bread. Garnish with basil leaves and sprinkle with pepper. Serve at once.

1 slender baguette

2 teaspoons olive oil

12 red and yellow cherry tomatoes, quartered

1 teaspoon balsamic vinegar

a pinch of sea salt

1 garlic clove, peeled

4–6 fresh basil leaves, plus extra to garnish

freshly ground black pepper

MAKES ABOUT 12

Sautéed mixed mushrooms with lemon herbed feta on toasted sourdough

Buttery mushrooms are a natural choice for breakfast, but they are also delicious stirred through pasta for an easy mid-week meal when you are low on time and energy.

Begin by making the herbed feta. Crumble the feta into a small mixing bowl. Add the lemon zest, parsley, thyme and 2 teaspoons of olive oil. Mash gently with a fork to combine and set aside.

To sauté the mushrooms, melt the butter and remaining 1 tablespoon of olive oil in a frying pan/skillet set over a high heat. Get the pan really hot without burning the butter before adding the mushrooms and garlic. Toss in the pan for a few minutes to coat the mushrooms, until they start to brown and crisp at the edges. Add a couple of good pinches of salt and freshly ground black pepper and allow the liquid in the mushrooms to evaporate, tossing the pan from time to time.

Add the spinach, stir through and remove the pan from the heat as it just starts to wilt. It will continue to cook from the heat of the mushrooms.

Toast the bread and pile each slice generously with the mushrooms and spinach. Crumble the herbed feta on top and serve.

60 g/½ cup feta

¼ teaspoon grated lemon zest

1 tablespoon fresh flat-leaf parsley, roughly chopped

2 sprigs of thyme, roughly chopped

2 teaspoons olive oil, plus 1 tablespoon for frying

30 g/2 tablespoons butter

400 g/6 cups mixed mushrooms (chesnut, flat, button, oyster), thickly sliced

1 garlic clove, crushed

sea salt and freshly ground black pepper

60 g/generous 1 cup spinach

4 slices sourdough bread

SERVES 2

Salads and summer soups

Vibrant, colourful plates of healthful
Mediterranean vegetables adorned with the
freshest herbs make for the very best hot-weather
dining. Refreshing bowls of soup can be most
reviving when only a light meal will do and so
satisfying enjoyed with a chunk of crusty bread.

Lemon, garlic and chilli potato salad

The potato salad is one of those all-time favourites at any picnic, and this version is no exception. The chilli/chile packs a punch with heat while the cooling lemon and herbs mingle with the garlic butter. Simply delicious.

Thoroughly wash the new potatoes under cold running water to remove any dirt, then put them in a large saucepan of water and bring to the boil. Cook for about 15–20 minutes, until the potatoes are tender.

While the potatoes are cooking, put the butter, garlic, lemon juice and chilli/chile in a small bowl and mix well.

Strain the potatoes and transfer them to a large mixing bowl, halving and quartering them as you go. Add the butter mixture to the bowl while the potatoes are still warm and gently stir to coat the potatoes in the butter. When the potatoes have cooled, sprinkle over the lemon zest and fresh herbs, season with salt and a little pepper and mix well again to thoroughly combine.

1 kg/2¹/₄ lbs. new potatoes, unpeeled

100 g/6¹/₂ tablespoons butter, softened

2 garlic cloves, crushed

freshly squeezed juice and grated zest of 2 lemons

1 long green chilli/chile, finely diced

a small handful of fresh flat-leaf parsley, roughly chopped

a small handful of fresh chives, roughly chopped

sea salt and freshly ground black pepper

SERVES 6

Catalan chickpea salad

Little earthenware bowls of this warm salad are seen in tapas bars all over Spain. It is satisfying and good, especially when mopped up with a chunk of crusty bread and served with a robust red wine or chilled lager. Although Spanish cooks would usually soak the dried chickpeas, then cook them with a little bit of pork, this chorizo version is easy and particularly delicious.

Heat the oil in a frying pan/skillet, add the onion, garlic, chorizo and bay leaves and sauté over gentle heat for 5 minutes or until softened but not browned. Stir in the pine nuts and chickpeas/garbanzo beans with a little of their liquid. Heat through until the flavours are combined, mashing a little with a fork.

Sprinkle with pepper and tomato and serve hot, warm or cool, but never chilled.

3 tablespoons extra virgin olive oil

1 red onion, sliced

2 garlic cloves, chopped

200 g/8 oz. cooking chorizo or other garlicky spiced pork sausage, sliced

2 bay leaves, bruised

2 tablespoons pine nuts, toasted in a dry frying pan/skillet

400 g/15 oz. canned chickpeas/garbanzo beans, drained, with 2 tablespoons of their liquid

coarsely ground black pepper

1 small tomato, finely chopped

SERVES 4

Black garlic tricolore salad

Insalata tricolore – Italy's patriotic red, white and green salad – is a classic which, when made with good-quality tomatoes, ripe avocado and fresh mozzarella, is such a treat to eat. Adding black garlic is an unorthodox touch, but the smoky sweetness of black garlic works well with the balsamic vinegar and gives an interesting flavour to the dish.

6 tablespoons extra virgin olive oil

2 tablespoons balsamic vinegar

2 black garlic cloves, finely chopped

3 mozzarella cheese balls, drained
    and sliced

4 ripe tomatoes, sliced

2 avocados, sliced and tossed with a little
    lemon juice to prevent discolouring

a handful of fresh basil leaves

sea salt and freshly ground black pepper

SERVES 4

Make the dressing by placing the olive oil, balsamic vinegar and black garlic in a small lidded jar, then shaking well to mix together. Season with salt and pepper.

Arrange the mozzarella, tomato and avocado in overlapping slices on a large serving plate. Pour over the black garlic dressing, scatter over the basil leaves and serve at once.

Tomato, freekeh and avocado salad

Freekeh's slightly chewy texture and nutty flavour contrasts nicely with the tomato and avocado in this simple, Middle Eastern-inspired salad. Serve as part of a buffet meal or as a side dish to cold roast chicken.

Cook the freekeh in a pan of boiling, salted water, simmering for 15–20 minutes until tender. Drain and allow to cool.

Using a sharp knife, cut the avocado in half, turning it as you do to cut around the stone/pit. Twist the two halves to separate. Remove the stone/pit and peel the two halves. Dice the flesh and toss with a little of the lemon juice to prevent any discolouration.

Mix together the cooked freekeh, cherry tomatoes, sun-dried tomatoes and spring onion/scallion. Toss with the oil, the remaining lemon juice and parsley. Fold in the diced avocado, top with pine nuts and serve at once.

100 g/²/₃ cup freekeh (a cracked, roasted green wheat)

1 ripe avocado

freshly squeezed juice of ¹/₂ lemon

12 cherry tomatoes, quartered

2 sun-dried tomatoes in oil, chopped

1 spring onion/scallion, finely chopped

2 tablespoons argan oil (or walnut oil)

2 tablespoons finely chopped fresh parsley

1 tablespoon pine nuts, toasted

SERVES 4

Panzanella

Perfect for a summertime lunch, this is a classic, rustic Tuscan recipe. Traditionally, it was made frugally with stale bread, given new life by being mixed with fresh tomatoes and flavourful olive oil.

1 red onion, very finely sliced into rings

100 ml/6 tablespoons white wine vinegar

2 teaspoons sugar

$^1/_2$ teaspoon sea salt

1 large yellow or red (bell) pepper

200 g/6$^1/_2$ oz. day-old rustic bread

500 g/1 lb. ripe tomatoes, ideally in assorted colours and shapes

100 ml/6 tablespoons extra virgin olive oil

50 ml/3 tablespoons red wine vinegar

1 garlic clove, crushed (optional)

1 teaspoon capers, rinsed

sea salt and freshly ground black pepper, to taste

a generous handful of fresh basil leaves

SERVES 6–8

First, lightly pickle the onion rings. Place them in a colander and pour over freshly boiled water. Transfer the onion rings to a mixing bowl and add the vinegar, sugar and salt. Pour over 150 ml/$^2/_3$ cup water and mix together. Set aside for 1 hour, drain and dry on paper towels.

Meanwhile, grill/broil the (bell) pepper under a medium heat until charred on all sides. Place in a plastic bag (as trapping the steam makes the pepper easier to peel) and set aside to cool. Peel using a sharp knife and cut into short, thick strips.

Trim and discard the crusts from the bread and slice into small cubes. Cut the tomatoes into chunks or in half if using small cherry tomatoes.

Make the dressing by mixing together the oil, red wine vinegar, garlic and capers. Season with salt and pepper, bearing in mind the saltiness of the capers.

Mix together the chopped tomatoes, bread and roasted pepper strips in a large serving bowl. Pour the dressing over the mixture and toss together, ensuring all the ingredients are well coated. Add the pickled onion rings, then the basil. Mix well and set aside for 15–20 minutes to allow the flavours to infuse before serving.

Tomato fattoush

Crisp pitta bread with juicy tomatoes and crunchy cucumber and radishes makes this version of a classic Lebanese mezze dish a salad to relish. Serve for a light meal or as an accompaniment to roasted lamb.

Slice the pitta around its edges to form two thin pitta halves. Brush with $^2/_3$ tablespoon of the oil and grill/broil under a medium heat for 2–3 minutes until golden-brown and crisp. Cool, then tear into small pieces.

Toss together the tomatoes, cucumber, radishes and spring onion/scallion in a serving bowl.

To make the dressing, mix together the remaining oil and the lemon juice, season with salt and pour over the salad. Mix in the crisp pitta bread pieces and parsley.

Sprinkle with sumac and serve at once.

1 pitta bread

$2^1/_2$ tablespoons extra virgin olive oil

500 g/1 lb. tomatoes, sliced thickly

$^1/_2$ cucumber, halved lengthways and sliced

6 radishes, finely sliced

1 spring onion/scallion, finely chopped

freshly squeezed juice of $^1/_2$ lemon

a pinch of sea salt

2 tablespoons freshly chopped flat-leaf parsley

2 teaspoons ground sumac

SERVES 4

Tomato, melon and feta salad

Perfect food for hot-weather dining. Sweet melon combined with juicy tomatoes and contrasted with salty feta, makes this a lovely dish. For a saltier contrast, substitute the feta with blue cheese and add sliced Parma ham. Serve with crusty bread to mop up every last drop of deliciousness.

Toss together all the melon and tomato pieces with the oil, vinegar and chives in a serving dish. Season well with pepper.

Gently mix in the feta cheese and serve at once.

Variation
Follow the instructions as above, replacing the feta with blue cheese. Stir in the shredded Parma ham/ prosciutto and serve at once.

$^1/_2$ Galia or other green-fleshed melon, peeled, deseeded and diced

$^1/_2$ cantaloupe melon, peeled, deseeded and diced

300 g/10 oz. tomatoes, sliced into wedges

2 tablespoons extra virgin olive oil

1 tablespoon sherry vinegar

2 tablespoons finely chopped fresh chives

freshly ground black pepper

100 g/3$^1/_2$ oz. feta cheese, diced

VARIATION

50 g/2 oz. blue cheese, such as Stilton or Gorgonzola, crumbled into pieces

3 slices of Parma ham/prosciutto, shredded

SERVES 4

Tomato tabbouleh

This zingy tomato and parsley salad is a Lebanese classic, traditionally served as a mezze dish. Gloriously refreshing, it goes well with grilled fish, chicken or lamb.

1 tablespoon bulgur wheat
350 g/12 oz. ripe but firm tomatoes
100 g/1 cup fresh flat-leaf parsley
1 spring onion/scallion, finely chopped
2 tablespoons finely sliced mint leaves
freshly squeezed juice of 1 lemon
2 tablespoons extra virgin olive oil
sea salt and freshly ground black pepper
fresh mint sprigs, to garnish

SERVES 4

Soak the bulgur wheat in cold water for 15 minutes to soften.

Meanwhile, finely dice the tomatoes, discarding the white stem base. Trim off and discard the stalks of the flat-leaf parsley and finely chop the leaves. If using a food processor, take care not to over-chop the parsley as it may turn to a pulp; you want the parsley to retain its texture.

Drain the soaked bulgur wheat, squeezing it dry of excess moisture. Toss together the diced tomatoes, chopped parsley, bulgur wheat, spring onion/scallion and mint. Add the lemon juice, oil, season with salt and pepper, and toss well.

Garnish the tabbouleh with mint and serve at once.

Sun-blush tomato, orange and burrata salad

Wonderfully simple to put together, this bright and colourful dish offers a Mediterranean-inspired combination of colours, textures and flavours.

Peel the oranges, making sure to trim off all the white pith, and cut into even, thick slices.

Place the orange slices on a large serving dish, then scatter over the sun-blush/semi-dried tomato halves. Tear the burrata cheeses into chunks and layer on top of the orange slices.

Drizzle with extra virgin olive oil and season with pepper.

Garnish with basil leaves and serve at once.

2 large oranges

24 sun-blush/semi-dried cherry tomato halves

2 burrata cheeses (or good-quality fresh mozzarella cheese)

TO SERVE
extra virgin olive oil
freshly ground black pepper
a handful of fresh basil leaves

SERVES 4

Heritage tomato and fennel salad

Good, fresh tomatoes need little else to showcase them. Choose the best, varied tomatoes you can find and enjoy them, simply.

Toast the flaked/slivered almonds in a small, dry heavy-bottomed frying pan/skillet until golden-brown. Swirl the pan regularly so that they don't burn. Remove from the pan and set aside.

Trim the fennel bulb, reserving the fronds, and slice very finely. Cut the tomatoes into thin slices.

Mix together the oil, lemon juice and smoked paprika/pimentón to make a dressing, seasoning with salt and pepper.

Arrange the fennel and tomato slices on a serving plate. Lightly toss with the dressing, sprinkle over the toasted almonds, garnish with the reserved fennel fronds and serve at once.

15 g/2 tablespoons flaked/slivered almonds

1 large fennel bulb

6–8 heritage tomatoes, ideally in assorted varieties

3 tablespoons extra virgin olive oil

1 tablespoon freshly squeezed lemon juice

1 teaspoon sweet smoked paprika/pimentón

sea salt and freshly ground black pepper

SERVES 4

Bresaola, oven tomatoes and buffalo mozzarella salad with mustard dressing

Bresaola is probably the best-known cured beef and it's a lovely way to enjoy beef. For many recipes, it combines even better with other flavours and ingredients than does cured pork, particularly in salads; it's generally a bit lighter in flavour and texture, so it works with the other ingredients rather than dominates them.

For the salad, first make the oven tomatoes. These tomatoes are best if made a day before, or at least given time to chill down in the refrigerator, so they become chewier and absorb the oil.

Preheat the oven to 180°C (350°F) Gas 4.

Put the halved tomatoes in a shallow ovenproof dish and drizzle the olive oil over the top. Tear the basil leaves over the tomatoes, then season with salt and pepper. Roast in the preheated oven for about 15–20 minutes, giving them a shimmy halfway through. Remove from the oven and let cool, then refrigerate.

When you are ready to serve, make the mustard dressing by simply combining the olive oil, vinegar, honey and mustard in a bowl, seasoning with salt and pepper, and mixing well.

Dress the salad leaves/greens with most of the dressing (reserving a little dressing for drizzling on top) and divide between 4 serving plates, then pop the torn mozzarella (or 8–9 mini mozzarella pearls/balls per serving), chilled oven tomatoes and bresaola slices on top, dividing them evenly between each plate. Drizzle the salads with the remaining dressing so that you get a taste of it even with the first mouthful, and serve immediately.

16–20 baby plum tomatoes, halved

1 tablespoon olive oil

a small bunch of fresh basil leaves (you want about 5–6 leaves per serving)

4 large handfuls of salad leaves/greens of your choice – such as baby leaf spinach and rocket/arugula

165 g/5½ oz. buffalo mozzarella cheese, drained and torn into pieces (or use 32–36 mini mozzarella cheese pearls/balls)

165 g/5½ oz. bresaola slices (about 20 average slices)

sea salt and freshly ground black pepper

DRESSING

2 tablespoons olive oil

2 tablespoons balsamic vinegar

1 tablespoon runny honey

1 teaspoon wholegrain mustard

SERVES 4

Prosciutto, artichoke, fig and roquefort salad with balsamic dressing

60 g/4 tablespoons butter

4 fresh figs (skin on), quartered

4 large handfuls of salad leaves/ greens
  of your choice (Little Gem/Bibb lettuce
  is very good for this salad)

125 g/4¼ oz. Roquefort cheese,
  crumbled

16–20 cooked artichoke hearts, chopped

165 g/5½ oz. prosciutto slices
  (about 20 average slices)

a small bunch of fresh basil leaves
  (about 5–6 leaves per serving)

sea salt and freshly ground black pepper

DRESSING

2 tablespoons olive oil

1 tablespoon balsamic vinegar

SERVES 4

A lovely, light summer salad — sweetness in the fig, saltiness in the prosciutto, and creamy Roquefort. A really simple balsamic dressing is fine to use here, as there are already plenty of flavours in the salad.

Preheat the grill/broiler to high.

For the salad, rub a little butter on all the cut surfaces of the figs, put them on a baking sheet, cut-sides up, and then pop them under the preheated grill/broiler for 6–8 minutes, turning once. Let them soften and start to brown, but don't let them shrivel up too much. Remove from the heat.

Meanwhile, make the dressing by combining the olive oil and vinegar in a bowl, seasoning with salt and pepper, and mixing well.

Dress the salad leaves/greens with most of the dressing (reserving a little dressing for drizzling on top) and divide between 4 serving plates, then pop the Roquefort, grilled figs, artichokes, prosciutto slices and basil leaves on top, dividing them evenly between each plate. Drizzle the salads with the remaining dressing and serve immediately.

Broad bean, feta and dill salad

The season for fresh, young broad/fava beans is short. They need very little preparation; just throw them into some boiling water, rinse, drain and add to pastas, risottos and salads, among other dishes. Older and frozen broad/fava beans can be used but they need a little more attention as their skins are tougher.

500 g/1 lb. shelled fresh young broad/
  fava beans or butter beans

65 ml/¼ cup olive oil

1 small red onion, finely chopped

2 garlic cloves, finely chopped

2 tablespoons freshly squeezed
  lemon juice

a small bunch of fresh dill, finely chopped

a handful of fresh flat-leaf parsley leaves

a handful of small fresh mint leaves

100 g/1 cup roughly crumbled feta cheese

freshly ground black pepper

SERVES 4

Cook the broad/fava beans in a large saucepan of boiling water for 10 minutes. Rinse under cold water and drain well. (If using older broad/fava beans, slip the skins off now and discard.)

Heat 1 tablespoon of the oil in a small frying pan/skillet set over a medium heat. Add the onion and garlic and cook for 2–3 minutes, until just softened.

Remove from the heat.

Put the broad/fava beans and herbs in a bowl. In a small bowl, use a fork to mix together the remaining oil and lemon juice and then pour over the salad.

Stir to combine. Add the feta, stir again, and season well with pepper before serving.

Spelt and spinach salad with pear and prosciutto

Pears and prosciutto are great vehicles for an excellent balsamic vinegar. The best ones come from Modena in Italy. This liquid gold is so good, you can eat it right from the spoon.

Soak the spelt berries in water overnight. Drain and put in a saucepan or pot. Pour in 450 ml/2 cups water (making sure there's enough to cover the spelt berries). Bring to the boil over a high heat then reduce the temperature, cover and simmer for 45 minutes. Remove the lid and drain if there is any excess water. Put in a separate bowl and leave to cool.

While the spelt berries are cooling, make the dressing by whisking 2 tablespoons of the balsamic vinegar together with the olive oil.

Dress the spelt berries with the balsamic vinaigrette and sprinkle in the fresh thyme leaves. Mix in the spinach. Season with salt and pepper.

To build the salad, scatter the spelt, spinach and thyme mixture on a serving plate. Layer the sliced pears and prosciutto on top.

Drizzle the extra 1½ tablespoons of balsamic vinegar over the pears and prosciutto and serve immediately.

200 g/1 cup spelt berries

460 ml/2 cups water

a handful of fresh thyme

100 g/4 cups baby spinach, chopped

2 pears, sliced

12 slices prosciutto or Parma ham

sea salt and freshly ground black pepper, to taste

DRESSING

3½ tablespoons balsamic vinegar

6 tablespoons olive oil

SERVES 4

Tomato, mozzarella and basil salad

Insalata Caprese, this classic salad born on the Isle of Capri, is hard to beat. It combines three ingredients that work totally in harmony with each other. The first is mozzarella, preferably soft, creamy mozzarella di bufala. Tomato — this must be red and ripe, and the same size as the ball of mozzarella — and basil, which must be fresh, pungent and plentiful. Although not strictly Italian, sliced avocado is a delicious addition. To make this salad really sing of sunny Capri, use the best possible ingredients and be generous with them.

Cut the mozzarella and tomatoes into slices about 5 mm/¼ in. thick. Arrange the tomato slices on a large plate and season with salt and pepper. Put 1 slice of mozzarella on each slice of tomato and top with a basil leaf. Tear up the remaining basil and scatter over the top.

Drizzle with a generous amount of olive oil just before serving.

This salad must be made at the last moment to prevent the tomatoes from weeping and the mozzarella from drying out. Serve at room temperature, never chilled, as this would kill the flavours.

2 balls of buffalo mozzarella cheese, 150 g/5 oz. each

2 large ripe tomatoes, roughly the same size as the balls of mozzarella

50 g/2 oz. fresh basil leaves

about 100 ml/½ cup extra virgin olive oil

sea salt and freshly ground black pepper

SERVES 4

Variation

If using avocado, halve and peel one ripe avocado, remove the stone and slice the flesh. Intersperse the slices of avocado with the tomato and mozzarella.

Grilled mixed vegetable salad with balsamic herb dressing

This is one of the easiest ways to cook and serve a selection of Mediterranean vegetables for a large number of people. Grilling the vegetables concentrates their flavours, and a touch of balsamic vinegar cuts through their sweetness. Don't cut the vegetables too small – this salad should be robust and chunky.

1 medium courgette/zucchini

1 medium aubergine/eggplant

1 large red (bell) pepper, halved and deseeded

12 tablespoons extra virgin olive oil

2 small red onions, quartered

150 g/6 oz. cherry tomatoes

2 teaspoons balsamic vinegar

1 garlic clove, crushed

3 tablespoons freshly chopped mixed herbs, such as parsley, basil, marjoram or oregano, plus extra to serve

sea salt and freshly ground black pepper

SERVES 4

Cut the courgette/zucchini, aubergine/eggplant and the pepper halves into large, bite-sized pieces. Transfer to a large bowl, add 6 tablespoons olive oil and toss well. Season to taste with salt and pepper.

Preheat the grill/broiler. Line a grill pan with foil and spoon in the vegetables. Add the onions and spread out the vegetables in an even layer (don't overcrowd the pan or they will stew). Grill under the preheated hot grill/broiler for 4–5 minutes or until the edges of the vegetables start to catch. Stir well, add the tomatoes and grill/broil for a further 5 minutes until the vegetables are browned and cooked but not mushy.

Meanwhile, whisk the remaining olive oil with the balsamic vinegar, garlic and herbs. Pour the dressing over the vegetables, toss lightly and transfer to a serving dish. Cover and set aside for at least 30 minutes to let the flavours infuse. Serve sprinkled with extra herbs. Do not serve this chilled as it would ruin the flavour.

Wild rice with artichoke, peaches and pine nuts

Wild rice is actually an edible grass, which has a slightly nutty and chewy flavour. It forms the base of a great grain salad — just add your favourite veggies and a simple vinaigrette.

Bring 1 litre/4 cups of water to the boil in a large saucepan or pot over a high heat. Add the wild rice, reduce the heat, cover and simmer for 45 minutes. Drain any excess water and set aside.

For the dressing, whisk together the walnut oil, lemon juice, salt and pepper in a large bowl.

Once the rice has cooled a bit but is still slightly warm, mix in the dressing with the artichokes, half of the coriander/cilantro, pine nuts and peaches.

Serve with an extra garnish of coriander/cilantro.

190 g/1 cup wild rice

400 g/1¹/₂ cups artichokes soaked in water (rinsed and drained)

a bunch of freshly chopped coriander/cilantro

30 g/¹/₄ cup pine nuts

60 g/¹/₂ cup chopped peaches

DRESSING

3 tablespoons walnut oil

2 tablespoons freshly squeezed lemon juice

¹/₂ teaspoon sea salt

¹/₂ teaspoon freshly ground black pepper

SERVES 2–4

Grilled squid with chorizo, feta and asparagus salad

Squid are tricky little beasts that take posthumous revenge on inexperienced chefs by only allowing the tiniest window in which to cook them properly. Too little, and they'll have a gelatinous, outer-space feel to them. Too much, and you might as well go and chew on the sole of your shoe. Chefs might wince at this, but as a general rule squid is best when grilled or deep-fried. The secret when grilling squid is to weigh it down on the grill, otherwise it will curl up in an instant, which will inevitably lead to some parts being undercooked and others rubberized. Use the bottom of a frying pan/skillet or a heavy roasting pan.

1 bunch asparagus (about 8 stalks)

180 g/6 oz. cooking chorizo, sliced

400 g/14 oz. squid (body and tentacles), cleaned

1 teaspoon hot paprika

2 tablespoons olive oil

100 g/3½ oz. feta cheese, crumbled

½ small bunch fresh flat-leaf parsley, roughly chopped

100 g/3½ oz. rocket/arugula

sea salt and freshly ground black pepper

1 lemon, cut into wedges, to serve

a ridged stove-top grill pan

SERVES 4

Bring a pan of salted water to the boil. Remove the woody stems from the asparagus and cook for about 3–4 minutes, until they bend easily but will still snap if forced. Refresh under cold running water and cut each spear into three pieces.

In a separate pan, fry the chorizo for 5 minutes, until cooked through, then set aside and leave to cool.

Preheat the ridged stove-top grill pan until smoking hot. Slit open the squid tubes so that you have flat 'sheets' of squid. Gently score them with a sharp knife in a diamond pattern.

Mix the paprika with a little olive oil and rub the mixture over the squid until it is completely covered. Season with salt and black pepper and place the squid flat on the hot grill, along with any tentacles. Put a frying pan/skillet or heavy roasting pan on top to stop the squid from curling up. Cook for about 1–2 minutes, depending on the thickness of your squid, then turn it over and cook for 1 more minute. Test a piece while it is cooking, just to be sure. It should offer just the slightest resistance to your bite. Remove from the pan and slice.

Combine the squid, asparagus, chorizo, feta, parsley and rocket/arugula on a plate, drizzle with a little olive oil and any cooking juices, and serve immediately with wedges of lemon.

Grilled tuna niçoise salad

Salad niçoise, if you're English, is made with canned tuna, boiled eggs and olives; if you're from other countries it can have anchovies instead of tuna or fresh tuna steak and some have potatoes and lettuce leaves too. All niçoise tend to have boiled eggs, olives, tomatoes, garlic and capers, so this version does, too. It also uses anchovies, waxy new potatoes and a tuna steak.

4 hard-boiled/hard-cooked eggs

sea salt and ground white pepper, to season

4 ripe red tomatoes, cut into wedges

a pinch of caster/granulated sugar

1 celery stalk, thinly sliced

50 g/¹/₂ cup pitted black olives, sliced into rounds

200 g/1¹/₂ cups small waxy new potatoes, boiled

¹/₂ cucumber

2 teaspoons capers

8 canned anchovies, sliced in half lengthways

4 spring onions/scallions, thinly sliced at an angle

a small bunch of fresh marjoram

4 tuna steaks (each about 120 g/4 oz.)

oil, to coat

PESTO

100 g/³/₄ cup pine nuts

2 garlic cloves, peeled

a small bunch of fresh basil

freshly squeezed juice of ¹/₂ lemon

a pinch of sea salt

olive oil, to drizzle

a ridged stovetop grill pan

SERVES 4

Begin by making the pesto; put the pine nuts, garlic and half of the basil in a food processor and pulse until combined but still with some texture. Add half of the lemon juice and the salt, and taste. Pour in a little oil to loosen the mixture, then add more basil and lemon as needed and pulse a couple more times, until the pesto can just be poured.

Next, prepare the salad. Peel and wedge the eggs, and season with a tiny amount of salt and white pepper. Sprinkle a tiny amount of sugar over the tomatoes and set aside for 5 minutes. Arrange the remaining ingredients except for the marjoram and tuna steaks on serving plates. Sprinkle with crushed marjoram leaves and drizzle each salad with a generous portion of the pesto.

Preheat a ridged stove-top grill pan over a high heat. Lightly oil the tuna steaks and season with a little salt. Place carefully on the pan and turn after 2–3 minutes, when the tuna is just charred and griddle lines are formed. Cook for another couple of minutes on the other side and serve on top of the salad.

Gazpacho with smoked salted croutons

1.3 kg/3 lbs. heirloom tomatoes
1 garlic clove
1 small red onion
2 Persian cucumbers
1 green (bell) pepper
1 Serrano chill/chile (red or green)
60 ml/¹/₄ cup extra virgin olive oil
60 ml/¹/₄ cup Jerez sherry vinegar
sel gris and coarsely ground black pepper
olive oil, to drizzle

SMOKED SALTED CROUTONS
1 small baguette
1 garlic clove, finely chopped
60 ml/¹/₄ cup olive oil
1 tablespoon smoked sea salt

SERVES 4

This recipe uses heirloom tomatoes of different colours, but if you can't find them, use any ripe and tasty tomatoes. The sherry vinegar is the key to gazpacho, so seek out a heady one from Jerez in Spain – it will make all the difference.

To peel the tomatoes, fill a small bowl with ice and water and set aside. Bring a medium-sized pan of water to the boil. Using a sharp knife, score a cross in the top of each tomato. Drop the tomatoes into the hot water for 30 seconds. Remove with a slotted spoon and drop into the iced water for 1 minute. Remove from the water and peel. Cut the tomatoes in half or quarters, depending on the size, and put in the food processor.

Roughly chop the garlic, onion and cucumbers and add to the tomatoes. Cut the green pepper and Serrano chilli/chile in half and remove the white pith and seeds. Chop and add to the tomatoes. Pulse the tomato mixture until it is chunky. Pour the gazpacho into a large bowl and stir in the olive oil and Jerez sherry vinegar. Season with sel gris and cracked black pepper then chill in the refrigerator until ready to serve.

Preheat the oven to 200°C (400°F) Gas 6.

To make the Smoked Salted Croutons, slice the baguette lengthways into 4 and lay the slices on a baking sheet. Mix the garlic and olive oil in a small bowl and drizzle over the bread. Sprinkle with the smoked sea salt and bake in the preheated oven for 8–10 minutes until golden.

Pour the gazpacho into 4 bowls and drizzle with olive oil. Serve with the Smoked Salted Croutons.

Ajo blanco with melon

Originating in Andalucía, the hot and arid part of southern Spain, it is perhaps no surprise that this elegant almond and garlic soup is served ice-cold. For the uninitiated, it may sound unusual, but it is delicious.

Cover the almonds with boiling water. Leave for 5 minutes, then one-by-one, pinch the almonds, squeezing them out of their skins (you can buy blanched almonds, but this method can improve the taste).

Place on a dry frying pan/skillet over a medium heat for a couple of minutes. You don't want to toast the almonds, just dry them out and tickle out their flavour with a bit of heat.

Add to a food processor with the bread, garlic and 2 level teaspoons of sea salt and blitz until very fine. When it is almost a paste, while still blitzing, drizzle in the olive oil very slowly until it is thick and smooth. Then slowly pour in the water and vinegar. Taste and adjust the seasoning if necessary with a little more vinegar, salt or olive oil. Refrigerate for at least 2 hours until thoroughly chilled.

Taste again prior to serving, as the flavours will change slightly as they get to know each other in the fridge. The soup will also thicken as it cools, so you can add in a few tablespoons of water if you want to thin it out a little. Ladle into chilled bowls and top with the wedges of melon. Drizzle over a little more extra virgin olive oil and serve immediately.

200 g/1¹⁄₃ cups whole almonds, skin on

50 g/2 oz. day-old bread, spelt or sourdough, crusts removed

3 small garlic cloves, peeled

sea salt

250 ml/1 cup good-quality extra virgin olive oil, plus extra to serve

420 ml/1¹⁄₂ cups ice-cold water

2 tablespoons sherry vinegar

1 melon, cantaloupe or charentais, cut into 4-cm/1¹⁄₂-in. wedges

SERVES 4–6

Spanish garlic soup

Garlic is at the heart of this rustic Spanish soup, sopa de ajo. The chicken stock is the key to its success, so if not making your own, buy the best quality stock you can find. Don't be tempted to use a stock cube!

First make the stock. Place all the stock ingredients in a large pan. Bring to the boil, then cover, reduce the heat and simmer for 1 hour. Strain and reserve the chicken stock.

To make the soup, heat the olive oil in a large saucepan. Add the garlic and fry gently, stirring, until it turns pale gold. Take care not to burn it, as this would make it bitter. Add the stock and season with salt. Bring to the boil, then reduce the heat and simmer for 10–15 minutes, until heated through. Stir in the paprika.

Toast or grill/broil the bread. Place a slice in each of four soup bowls, pour over the soup, garnish with parsley and serve at once.

2 tablespoons olive oil

4 garlic cloves, sliced

sea salt

1 teaspoon sweet Spanish paprika

4 slices of rustic bread

chopped fresh parsley, to garnish

CHICKEN STOCK

700 g/1¹⁄₂ lbs. chicken wings

1.2 litres/5 cups water

1 onion, chopped

1 carrot, chopped

2 celery sticks, chopped

1 garlic clove, peeled

5 peppercorns

(or 1 litre/4¹⁄₄ cups good-quality chicken stock)

SERVES 4

250 g/8 oz. day-old sourdough bread

1 kg/2¼ lbs. ripe tomatoes

2 tablespoons olive oil

2 garlic cloves, peeled and crushed

sea salt and freshly ground black pepper

150 ml/²/₃ cup tomato passata/strained
    tomatoes

150 ml/²/₃ cup hot water

leaves from a small bunch of fresh basil

2 tablespoons extra virgin olive oil,
    plus extra to serve

SERVES 4–6

Preheat the oven to 100°C (215°F) Gas ¼.

Slice the bread thickly and trim off the crusts. Place the bread in the oven for 15–20 minutes in order to dry it out, then set aside.

Next, scald the tomatoes. Pour boiling water over the ripe tomatoes in a heatproof bowl. Set aside for 1 minute, then drain and carefully peel off the skin using a sharp knife. Roughly chop, reserving any juices, and set aside.

Heat the olive oil in a large, heavy-bottomed saucepan or pot set over a medium heat. Add the garlic and fry gently, stirring continuously for 2 minutes, until fragrant. Add the chopped tomatoes with their juices, stir and season with salt and pepper. Bring the mixture to the boil, reduce the heat and simmer uncovered for 30 minutes, stirring now and then to break down the tomatoes. Add the tomato passata/strained tomatoes and hot water, mix well and simmer for a couple of minutes.

Tear the dried bread into small pieces and mix into the tomato soup, so that it thickens, resembling porridge in texture. Mix in the basil leaves and extra virgin olive oil.

Serve with a drizzle of extra virgin olive oil over each serving.

Pappa al pomodoro

A classic Tuscan dish, pappa al pomodoro is based, with characteristic frugality, on simple ingredients – dry bread, ripe tomatoes, olive oil and fragrant basil – transformed into a flavourful, thick-textured 'soup'. As with all Italian cuisine, using quality ingredients is key, so choose good bread, the juiciest of tomatoes and a fine extra virgin olive oil.

Tomato soup with fennel, garlic and basil drizzle

Tomato and basil are a classic summer flavour combination. The green basil oil provides a vibrant colour contrast to the orange-red of the soup base and elevates this humble tomato soup to something a little more refined.

Preheat the oven to 200°C (400°F) Gas 6.

To roast the garlic, cut the top part off the top of the garlic head to expose the individual garlic cloves. Place the garlic head, cut-side down, onto a square piece of foil and drizzle with 2 teaspoons of olive oil. Lift the foil up around the garlic and place on a baking sheet. Roast in the preheated oven for 45 minutes. Remove from the oven, open the foil wrap and set aside to cool. When the garlic is cool enough to handle, squeeze the cloves out of the skin, coarsely chop the garlic flesh and discard the skin.

Place the quartered fennel in a roasting pan, drizzle with 1 tablespoon of olive oil and season with the salt and freshly ground black pepper. Cook in the same oven as the garlic for 25 minutes, or until you can easily insert the tip of a sharp knife into the flesh. Remove from the oven, set aside to cool slightly then roughly chop.

To make the Basil Oil, whizz together a little of the olive oil with the fresh basil and salt in a food processor. With the motor running, slowly drizzle in more oil until you have a loose, flavoured oil. Set aside until ready to serve.

Heat 2 tablespoons of olive oil in a large saucepan or pot set over a medium heat. Add the chopped leek, celery and carrot and gently cook for 10–15 minutes, stirring from time to time, until the vegetables are soft.

Add the roast garlic and fennel, fresh and canned tomatoes and vegetable stock. Bring the mixture to the boil then reduce the heat and simmer for 45 minutes.

Remove the pan from the heat, stir in the basil leaves and purée with a hand-held electric mixer or in a food processor.

Season to taste and serve with a good drizzle of basil oil, some freshly ground black pepper, and garnish with fresh basil leaves.

1 head of garlic

olive oil, for roasting

350 g/10 oz. (about 1 large) fennel bulb, trimmed and quartered

sea salt and freshly ground black pepper, to season

1 leek (white part only), roughly chopped

100 g/³/4 cup (about 2 sticks) chopped celery

150 g/1¹/4 cups (about 1 medium) chopped carrot

500 g/2¹/2 cups (about 4 medium) roughly chopped tomatoes

1 x 400-g/14-oz. can plum tomatoes

500 ml/2 cups vegetable stock

15 g/¹/4 cup fresh basil

BASIL OIL

150 ml/²/3 cup olive oil, plus extra if needed

60 g/1 cup fresh basil

sea salt, to taste

SERVES 4

Tuscan bean soup with rosemary

Toscanelli are the small beans grown and eaten by the Tuscan mangiafagioli (bean eaters). It is a simple soup to be found in various guises all over central and northern Italy. To give it a sophisticated touch fry sliced garlic, rosemary and chilli/chile in really good olive oil, just enough to release their aromas, and spoon this over the soup just before serving. The aroma is intoxicating. Like many other rugged soups, it is often served as a main course ladled over toasted country bread.

250 g/1¹/₂ cups dried white or brown beans (such as haricot, borlotti or cannellini)

a pinch of bicarbonate of/baking soda

cold water, or chicken or vegetable stock (see method)

a handful of fresh sage leaves, plus 2 tablespoons chopped fresh sage

4 garlic cloves

300 ml/1¹/₄ cups olive oil

2 tablespoons freshly chopped rosemary

a large pinch of dried chilli/red pepper flakes

sea salt and freshly ground black pepper

coarsely chopped fresh flat-leaf parsley, to serve

SERVES 6

Put the beans in a bowl, cover with cold water, add a pinch of bicarbonate of/baking soda, soak overnight, then drain just before you're ready to use them.

Preheat the oven to 160°C (325°F) Gas 3.

Put the drained beans in a flameproof casserole. Cover with cold water or chicken or vegetable stock to a depth of 5 cm/2 in. above the beans, and push in the handful of sage. Bring to the boil, cover tightly with a lid and transfer to the preheated oven for about 1 hour or until tender. (The time depends on the freshness of the beans – test after 40 minutes.) Keep them in their cooking liquid.

Meanwhile, finely chop 2 of the garlic cloves, and thinly slice the remainder. Put half the beans, the cooked sage (minus any stalks), and all the liquid into a blender or food processor and blend until smooth. Pour back into the remaining beans in the casserole. If the soup is thicker than you like, add extra water or stock to thin it down.

Heat half the olive oil in a frying pan/skillet and add the chopped garlic. Fry gently until soft and golden, then add the chopped sage and cook for 30 seconds. Stir this into the soup and reheat until boiling. Simmer gently for 10 minutes. Add salt and pepper to taste.

Pour into a heated tureen or soup bowls. Heat the remaining olive oil in a small frying pan/skillet, add the sliced garlic and fry carefully until golden (don't let it go too dark or it will be bitter). Stir in the rosemary and dried chilli/red pepper flakes. Dip the base of the frying pan/skillet in cold water to stop the garlic cooking. Spoon the garlic and oil over the soup, then serve sprinkled with chopped fresh parsley.

ROSEMARY OIL

2 tablespoons olive oil

1 sprig fresh rosemary

MUSSELS

1¹/₃ tablespoons olive oil

1 white onion, chopped

500 g/1 lb. 2 oz. mussels, cleaned

50 ml/scant ¹/₄ cup white wine

SOUP BASE

2 tablespoons olive oil

60 g/2¹/₄ oz. cubed pancetta

30 g/2 tablespoons butter

2 garlic cloves, chopped

2 celery sticks, chopped

2 white onions, chopped

2 small carrots, chopped

a small bunch of fresh flat-leaf parsley, leaves and stalks chopped

2 sprigs fresh rosemary, stalks removed

2 x 400-g/14-oz. cans cannellini beans in water

a hand-held electric blender or jug blender

SERVES 2

Everyone's so busy fretting about how to cook a live lobster humanely that they've forgotten all about the countless mussels being steamed alive every day. This satisfying soup is divine served on a sunny day or tastes just as good at any time of the year.

Mussel, cannellini and pancetta soup with rosemary oil

Prepare the rosemary oil by putting the olive oil and the rosemary (stalks included) in a frying pan/skillet. Warm over medium heat until the rosemary has darkened. Set aside to cool.

For the mussels, heat the olive oil in a deep pan set over a high heat and add the onion. Fry for about 5 minutes, until lightly caramelized, then add the mussels and white wine. Cover with a lid and steam over high heat until the shells have opened. Set a colander over a bowl and drain the mussels, being sure to keep the liquid for later. Discard any mussels that remain closed. Keep a few to one side for decorating the dish, remove the rest from their shells and set aside.

For the soup base, warm a heavy-based pan over medium heat and add the oil and pancetta. Fry the pancetta until the fat has rendered and the cubes are nicely crispy, then remove them with a slotted spoon and set aside. Add the butter, garlic, celery, onions, carrots, parsley and rosemary. Gently fry for 10 minutes, until beginning to brown. Add the cannellini beans along with their water and the reserved juice from cooking the mussels. Cover and cook over low heat for 20 minutes, or until the beans are beginning to disintegrate. Liquidize the soup with a hand-held electric blender or jug blender until it is a smooth, unctuous consistency. Add the fried pancetta, shelled mussels and a few turns of the pepper mill and season with salt to taste.

Serve with a generous drizzle of rosemary oil and a few mussels in their shells to decorate.

Bouillabaisse

1 baguette, sliced diagonally into 5-mm/$1/4$-in. slices, lightly toasted

4 hake steaks (each about 100 g/$31/2$ oz.)

8 extra-large/colossal prawns/shrimp, shells and heads on

800 g/$13/4$ lbs. mussels, cleaned

200 g/$11/2$ cups peeled and cooked small new potatoes

50 ml/$31/2$ tablespoons Pernod (or other aniseed-based liqueur)

sea salt, to season

150 g/$51/2$ oz. smoked or cured salmon

freshly chopped flat-leaf parsley

FISH STOCK

4 brown onions, roughly chopped

8 carrots, thinly sliced

2 tomatoes, cut into quarters

the peel of 1 lemon

2 litres/$31/2$ pints cold water

1 kg/$21/4$ lbs. fish bones

100 g/$11/2$ cups uncooked prawns/shrimp, shells on

SAUCE

1 brown onion, sliced

2 garlic cloves, sliced

a pinch of saffron threads

$1/2$ fennel bulb, sliced

olive oil

1 red (bell) pepper

300 ml/$11/4$ cups Fish Stock

1 teaspoon caster/granulated sugar

a small bunch of fresh thyme, sage and bay, tied into a bouquet garni

500 g/18 oz. fish heads (if available)

800 g/4 cups canned chopped tomatoes

ROUILLE

200 ml/$3/4$ cup mayonnaise

2 garlic cloves, crushed

a small pinch of saffron threads

SERVES 4

The king of all fish dishes, this French Provençal dish is not for the faint-hearted as there are bones and shells to pick through, it is proper finger food, definitely not a dish to wear a white shirt to eat. The name 'bouillabaisse' comes from the phrases 'to boil' and 'to simmer'. The fish should be boiled in salty water, then simmered in a tomato-based stock. Triple the quantities to transform this into a summer feast for ten people – it makes a great talking point and is a magnificent celebration of seafood.

To make the fish stock, put all of the ingredients in a large pan set over a gentle—medium heat, bring to a low simmer and cook for 15 minutes. Reduce heat and continue to cook for a further 45 minutes. Pour the liquid through a fine sieve/strainer into a jug/pitcher and discard the pulp.

For the sauce, put the onion, garlic, saffron and fennel in a large saucepan with a generous amount of oil (about 5 mm/$1/4$ in. deep) and cook over a low heat for about 5 minutes to brown everything slightly.

Carefully place the (bell) pepper over a naked flame on a gas stovetop to blacken, turning once (if you do not have a gas stovetop, place under a grill/broiler on a high heat for 5 minutes). Peel away most of the skin, then slice the flesh and add to the sauce.

Add the fish stock, sugar, bouquet garni, fish heads and tomatoes and bring to a low simmer for 45 minutes.

Remove the fish heads and bouquet garni then purée using a hand-held electric blender to a smooth liquid. Store the sauce in the fridge or freezer – it actually improves if stored for a day in the fridge.

Next, make the rouille by mixing the mayonnaise, garlic and saffron together in a large mixing bowl using a hand-held electric blender. Set aside.

Toast the bread slices under a medium grill/broiler until lightly golden. Set aside until ready to serve.

For the bouillabaise, bring a pan of heavily salted water to a simmer and add the hake. Cook for 4 minutes until opaque and just starting to break up.

Lift the hake from the water and put in a large saucepan with the prawns/shrimp, mussels, potatoes and chilled sauce. Set over a medium heat and bring to a low simmer for 5 minutes. Add the Pernod and stir gently, then taste and season with salt, if needed.

Pour the bouillabaisse into deep bowls, arranging the fish and shellfish for presentation. Top each with cured salmon and sprinkle with chopped parsley. Serve with the rouille, baguette and a side plate for bones and shells.

Sunshine lunches

Whether lunching by the coast listening to the ocean waves lapping on the shore, picnicking on the warm sand or simply dreaming of sunnier climes, there's a lunch here for you. There's the finest fish dishes from a stunning tuna and melon tartare to harissa sardines with tomato salad, or more portable feasts such as a Spanish tortilla omelette, roast garlic focaccia and summer tomato tart.

Spanish potato omelette

Spain's celebrated thick tortilla omelette (tortilla de patata) is one of the world's most accommodating dishes: good for any occasion and particularly useful as a portable picnic food, a quick lunch dish eaten between slices of bread. Served with this scarlet piquillo sauce, it is delicious.

100 ml/¹/₃ cup extra virgin olive oil

1 k/2¹/₄ lbs. salad potatoes, peeled and cut into 2-cm/³/₄-in. cubes

1 onion, sliced into rings

4 garlic cloves, finely chopped (optional)

6 eggs, beaten

4 tablespoons freshly-chopped flat-leaf parsley or spring onion/scallion tops

sea salt and freshly ground black pepper

PIQUILLO SAUCE

225-g/8-oz. can or jar of roasted piquillo peppers or pimientos

3 tablespoons sherry vinegar

SERVES 4–6

Heat the oil in a medium frying pan/skillet, add the potatoes and onion and cook over low heat for 12–14 minutes or until tender but not browned, moving them about with a fish slice so that they cook evenly. Add the garlic, if using, for the last 2 minutes.

Put the eggs, salt and pepper in a bowl and beat well.

Using a slotted spoon, remove the cooked potatoes and garlic from the pan and stir it into the egg mixture. Stir in the chopped parsley.

Quickly pour the egg mixture back into the hot frying pan/skillet. Cook, without stirring, over low to moderate heat for 4–5 minutes or until firm, but

do not let it brown too much. The top will still be wobbly, only part-cooked.

Holding a heatproof plate over the top of the omelette, quickly invert the pan, omelette and plate. Slide the hot omelette back, upside down, to brown the other side for 2–3 minutes more, then remove from the pan and leave to cool for 5 minutes.

To make the sauce, put the piquillo, 6 tablespoons of the liquid from the can (make it up with water if necessary) and the sherry vinegar in a blender. Purée to form a smooth, scarlet sauce.

Cut the omelette into chunks, segments or cubes. Serve the sauce separately, spooning some over the pieces of tortilla.

Note

In many Spanish bars and cafés, sliced courgettes/zucchini, spinach, onion or red (bell) peppers may be added to the potatoes for variety, flavour and colour, but plain potato is the most common and well loved.

Sliced coppa and spring onion frittata

Frittata – the Italian omelette. This is lovely and rich with the cheese and meat. Wonderful when served with a Pinot Grigio to balance the richness.

20 g/generous 1 tablespoon butter

8–10 spring onions/scallions, sliced

6 eggs, beaten

2 tablespoons milk

a big pinch of freshly chopped parsley

1 tablespoon crème fraîche/sour cream

60 g/2¹/₄ oz. soft goats' cheese (or soft cheese of your choice)

100 g/3³/₄ oz. coppa or salami, sliced

sea salt and freshly ground black pepper

salad leaves/greens, to serve

2 lemon quarters, to serve (optional)

SERVES 2

Heat the butter in a frying pan/skillet until melted, then fry the spring onions/scallions over high heat, until soft and browned. Meanwhile, mix the eggs with the milk, parsley and some salt and pepper. Pour the beaten egg mixture over the spring onions/scallions and stir once to mix well. Turn the heat down to medium and leave the egg mixture to cook (without stirring) until it starts to thicken.

Meanwhile, preheat the grill/broiler to high.

Once the bottom of the frittata starts to set in the frying pan/skillet, put the crème fraîche/sour cream on the top of the frittata in evenly spaced 'dollops'.

Do the same with the pieces of goats' cheese and then with the slices of coppa, pushing the middle of the slices down slightly so the sides fold up.

Transfer the frying pan/skillet to the preheated grill/broiler and grill/broil for about 5 minutes, until the top browns.

Keep checking the frittata regularly to make sure it doesn't burn.

Serve immediately, sliced into wedges. Serve with a side of dressed salad leaves/greens and a lemon quarter to squeeze over the top, if you like.

Pancake 'calzones'

A savoury folded pancake with mortadella, mozzarella (or Gorgonzola) and fried Mediterranean vegetables with pesto. This recipe is a twist on a traditional calzone (made with pizza dough) but is much less filling and also brings out the flavours of the mortadella.

PANCAKE BATTER

40 g/^{1}/$_3$ cup plain/all-purpose flour

a pinch of sea salt

1 egg, beaten

50 ml/scant ^{1}/$_4$ cup milk

20 g/generous 1 tablespoon butter

FILLING

1 garlic clove, finely chopped

6–7 button/white mushrooms, sliced

1 courgette/zucchini, thinly sliced

1 tablespoon olive oil

4–5 sun-dried tomatoes, chopped

200-g/7-oz. can of tomatoes, drained

1 tablespoon tomato purée/paste

1 tablespoon pesto

a handful of fresh basil leaves

200 g/7 oz. mortadella, torn into pieces

200 g/7 oz. mozzarella cheese, torn (or use Gorgonzola, crumbled, for a richer feast)

sea salt and freshly ground black pepper

MAKES 2

To make the batter, sift the flour and salt into a bowl, then whisk/beat in the egg, milk and 1 tablespoon cold water to make a smooth batter. Cover and leave in the refrigerator whilst you prepare the filling.

For the filling, fry the garlic, mushrooms and courgette/zucchini with the olive oil in a frying pan/skillet over medium heat, until brown, then add the sun-dried tomatoes, canned tomatoes, tomato purée/paste, pesto and basil leaves, season with salt and pepper, and stir until hot. Remove from the heat and keep hot.

Meanwhile, make the pancakes. Heat another frying pan/skillet over medium heat and melt half the butter. Once the butter is melted, pour half of the batter evenly into the pan, swirling it around to coat the bottom of the pan, and leave to cook.

Once the bottom is cooked, flip the pancake over, then spoon half of the vegetable mixture onto one side of the pancake. Quickly add half of the mortadella and mozzarella, then fold the pancake over and keep it over low heat for 1–2 minutes more, until the cheese has melted. Repeat with the remaining butter, batter and vegetables to make a second calzone. Serve immediately.

Tomato Parmesan frittata

Serve this Italian tomato-flavoured omelette as a light lunch with a crisp green salad and crusty bread.

Halve the tomatoes, scoop out and discard the soft pulp and seeds, forming tomato shells. Thinly slice them and set aside.

Heat the oil in a heavy-bottomed frying pan/skillet set over a low heat. Add the onion and fry, stirring now and then, for 5 minutes until softened. Add the tomato slices and season with salt and pepper. Increase the heat and fry, stirring often, for 5 minutes until softened and pulpy. Set aside to cool.

Beat the eggs in a large mixing bowl and stir in the Parmesan cheese and parsley. Season with a little salt and pepper. Mix in the cooled tomato mixture.

Heat the butter in the ovenproof frying pan/skillet over a medium–high heat, until frothy. Pour in the egg mixture, reduce the heat to low and cook gently for around 25 minutes.

Meanwhile, preheat the grill/broiler to a medium heat.

Place the frittata under the hot grill/broiler and cook for 3 minutes, until set and browned. Slice into quarters and serve hot or at room temperature.

450 g/1 lb. ripe tomatoes

1 tablespoon olive oil

1 onion, finely sliced

sea salt and freshly ground black pepper

5 eggs

2 tablespoons freshly grated Parmesan cheese

2 tablespoons finely chopped fresh flat-leaf parsley

25 g/1½ tablespoons butter

a 20-cm/8-in. ovenproof frying pan/skillet

SERVES 4

Spanish tart with peppers

This Spanish tart is often enjoyed in tapas bars, cut into uneven chunks and piled high on little plates, served with olives and glasses of the local wine.

To make the dough, put the flour, yeast and salt in a bowl and mix. Add the water and mix to a satiny dough, then knead, still in the bowl for 5 minutes or until silky. Cover the bowl with a cloth and leave for about 1 hour or until the dough has doubled in size.

Meanwhile, to make the topping, heat 3 tablespoons of the oil in a frying pan/skillet, add the onions and cook, stirring over medium heat until softened and transparent. Slice half the piquillos and add to the pan. Stir in most of the herbs. Preheated the oven to 220°C (425°F) Gas 7.

Transfer the dough to a heavy, dark, oiled baking sheet. Punch down, flatten and roll out the dough to a circle 30 cm/12 in. diameter. Snip, twist or roll the edges. Spread the anchovy paste all over the top. Add the remaining piquillos, left whole, and the cooked onion mixture. Arrange the anchovies and remaining herbs in a decorative pattern on top and sprinkle with the remaining oil.

Bake in the preheated oven for 25–30 minutes until the base is crisp and risen, the edges golden and the filling hot and wilted. Serve in wedges, hot or cool.

250 g/1⅓ cups plain/all-purpose flour

½ sachet dried/active dry yeast, 3.5 g/⅛ oz.

½ teaspoon sea salt

150 ml/⅔ cup lukewarm water

TOPPING

4 tablespoons extra virgin olive oil

350 g/12 oz. red onions, cut into wedges

about 500 g/1 lb. canned piquillo peppers, drained

leaves from a small handful of fresh thyme or rosemary sprigs

2 tablespoons anchovy paste or purée, or canned anchovies, chopped and mashed

16 marinated anchovy fillets

a baking sheet, greased

SERVES 4–6

Ricotta tarts with pea and mint

These fresh and tasty tarts not only look beautiful, but also give you the opportunity to make your own cheese, which is simple and fun to do.

250 g/9 oz. puff pastry

200 g/7 oz. ricotta or curd cheese (see below)

100 g/³/₄ cup frozen peas

a bunch of fresh mint

1 egg, beaten

sea salt and freshly ground black pepper, to season

CURD CHEESE

1.5 litres/quarts whole milk

2 teaspoons table salt

2 tablespoons white wine vinegar

a 15-cm/6-in. diameter baking ring

SERVES 4

Preheat the oven to 180°C (350°F) Gas 4.

Roll out the puff pastry on a lightly floured surface to a thickness of about 3 mm/⅛ in.

Using the baking ring as a guide and a small, sharp knife, cut eight pastry circles. Do not press the circles out using the ring, or the edges will be pinched together and the pastry will not rise.

On four of the circles, cut a second circle out of the middle, about 10 cm/ 4 in. in diameter. This will leave you with four rings of puff pastry.

Now you need to stick the rings onto the remaining circles, which will form the tarts. Lightly moisten one side of the rings with a little water and place them on top of the circles. Gently, transfer to a baking sheet.

Brush the rings with a little beaten egg and, using a fork, poke small holes in the centre circle of each tart. Sprinkle with a little sea salt and bake in the preheated oven for 10 minutes, until the tops are risen and have turned golden. Remove from the oven and allow to cool. Reduce the heat to 140°C (275°F) Gas 1.

In a large mixing bowl, gently mash the ricotta or curd cheese, peas and a few leaves of chopped mint together. Spoon the mixture into the tart cases. Overfill the cases, so the mixture is spilling over the top. Return to the cooled oven for 20 minutes.

Remove, sprinkle with black pepper, decorate with a couple of mint leaves and serve immediately.

How to make curd cheese

Pour the milk into a saucepan. Add the table salt and set over a medium heat. Bring the milk to about 70°C (190°F) when tested using a temperature probe. Add the white wine vinegar and stir gently. The milk should start to curdle. Leave the milk for a couple of minutes to separate into curds and whey.

Line a fine mesh sieve/strainer with a fine cloth, muslin/cheesecloth or clean kitchen cloth and set over a large mixing bowl. Strain the mixture through this – you should be left with about 250 g/ 9 oz. of curds in the sieve/strainer.

Set in a fridge, leaving the curds in the sieve/strainer over the bowl, to completely drain for about 1 hour. Remove from the fridge and twist your cloth around the strained curds to press them together, forming a simple cheese, which is ready to use.

Summer tomato tart

Gloriously simple to make, this Mediterranean-flavoured tart tastes as good as it looks. If available, use different coloured tomatoes for the topping for extra visual appeal. Serve for a light meal accompanied by a crisp green side salad.

300 g/10 oz. puff pastry
450 g/1 lb. ripe tomatoes
2 tablespoons black olive tapenade
sea salt and freshly ground black pepper
a handful of fresh basil leaves, to garnish
a baking sheet, greased

SERVES 6

On a lightly floured surface, thinly roll out the puff pastry to form a circle about 27 cm/11 in. in diameter. Chill the pastry circle in the fridge for 30 minutes.

Preheat the oven to 200°C (400°F) Gas 6.

Cut the tomatoes into 5-mm/¼-in. thick slices.

Place the chilled pastry circle on the prepared baking sheet. Spread the olive tapenade evenly over the pastry, leaving a 2-cm/¾-in. rim around the edge. Arrange the tomato slices in spiralling rings over the tapenade, overlapping them slightly. Season with a little salt and pepper, bearing in mind the saltiness of the tapenade.

Bake in the preheated oven for 40 minutes, then reduce the oven temperature to 150°C (300°F) Gas 2 and bake for a further 1 hour, until the pastry is crisp and golden-brown and the tomatoes are cooked through.

Serve either warm from the oven or at room temperature, garnished with basil leaves.

Stuffed aubergines/eggplants

In Greek, this dish is called 'papoutsakias', which means 'little shoes' and these stuffed aubergines/eggplants do in fact look like slippers. They are often flavoured with leaves from the pot of basil seen on Greek window sills, but this recipe uses oregano, that favourite of all Greek herbs. The local kind, known as rigani, grows wild everywhere and seems to have more verve than any other variety.

Preheat the oven to 180°C (350°F) Gas 4.

Using a sharp, serrated knife, cut out the central flesh of the aubergine/eggplant halves, leaving a 1 cm/½ in. shell. Cut the flesh into 1-cm/½-in. chunks. Heat 4 tablespoons of the oil in a large frying pan/skillet, add the garlic and aubergine/eggplant halves cut sides down. Cook over moderate heat for 5 minutes. Remove and set the aubergine/eggplant halves, cut side up, in a baking dish, ready to be filled. Leave the oil and garlic in the pan.

Put the aubergine/eggplants halves in the preheated oven for 15 minutes while you prepare the filling and sauce.

Add the aubergine/eggplant cubes to the oil in the pan. Sauté for 5 minutes, then add the onion, tomatoes, celery, if using, and the dried oregano and cook over high heat. Add the remaining oil and cook, stirring constantly, until the aubergine/eggplant chunks are fairly soft and the tomatoes reduced. Scoop up the aubergine/eggplant pieces with some of the other vegetables and pile them inside the part-cooked shells and bake them for a further 40 minutes.

Meanwhile, add the tomato purée/paste to the pan, then add the boiling water. Stir over gentle heat for a further 15 minutes to form a rich, soft, fragrant sauce, then turn off the heat. Taste and season well with salt and pepper.

After 1 hour in the oven, test the aubergines/eggplants: the outer shells should be dark, wrinkled and soft. If not, cook them for another 20 minutes. Serve the aubergines/eggplants in their baking dish or a serving plate, with the sauce poured over and around. Top with the fresh herbs and cheese, if using.

2 large aubergines/eggplants, about 600–700 g/1½ lbs. halved lengthways

6 tablespoons extra virgin olive oil

6 garlic cloves, crushed

1 red or white onion, sliced into rings

6 firm-fleshed ripe red tomatoes, blanched, skinned, then cut into segments

2 celery sticks, chopped (optional)

1 teaspoon dried oregano

4 tablespoons thick tomato purée/paste

175 ml/¾ cup boiling water

sprigs of fresh oregano, marjoram or thyme (optional)

4 thin slices cheese, such as Greek kasseri, Cheddar or pecorino, about 50 g /2 oz. (optional)

sea salt and freshly ground black pepper

a baking dish big enough to hold the aubergines/eggplants in a single layer

SERVES 4

Aubergines/eggplants stuffed with onions and tomatoes

Whether the Imam fainted from shock or pleasure as a result of the quantity of olive oil used in this dish, no one knows, but the 'Imam fainted' is the name of this mezza classic, 'imam bayıldı'. Olive oil plays a central role in a number of Ottoman vegetable dishes, which are cooked in the oil for flavour and are always served cold. These deliciously tender aubergines/eggplants can be baked in the oven or gently poached.

4 medium-sized aubergines/ eggplants

sunflower oil

2 onions, halved lengthways and finely sliced

4 tomatoes, skinned (see page 55), deseeded and roughly chopped

2–3 garlic cloves, finely chopped

a bunch of fresh flat-leaf parsley, finely chopped (reserve a little for garnishing)

a bunch of fresh dill, finely chopped (reserve a little for garnishing)

1 teaspoon sea salt

150 ml/1¹⁄₃ cups olive oil

50 ml/3 tablespoons water

freshly squeezed juice of 1 lemon

1 tablespoon granulated sugar

lemon wedges, to serve

SERVES 4

Using a sharp knife or a potato peeler, peel the aubergines/ eggplants in stripes like a zebra. Place them in a bowl of salted water for 5 minutes, then pat them dry. Heat up enough sunflower oil for frying in a frying pan/skillet. Place the aubergines/eggplants in the oil and fry for 2–3 minutes, rolling them over in the oil, to soften and lightly brown them – the oil will spit, so have a lid at hand.

Transfer the softened aubergines/eggplants to a wide, shallow pan, placing them side by side, and slit them open, keeping the ends and bottom intact, so that they resemble hollowed-out canoes.

In a bowl, mix together the onions, tomatoes, garlic and herbs. Add the salt and a little of the olive oil. Spoon the onion and tomato mixture into the aubergine/eggplant pockets, packing it in tightly, so that all of it is used up.

Mix together the rest of the olive oil with the water and lemon juice, pour it over the aubergines/eggplants, and sprinkle the sugar over the top.

Cover the pan with a lid and place it over a medium heat to get the oil hot and create some steam. Reduce the heat and cook the aubergines/eggplants gently for about 40 minutes, basting them from time to time, until they are soft and tender and only a little oil is left in the bottom of the pan. Leave them to cool in the pan.

Carefully lift the stuffed aubergines/eggplants onto a serving dish and spoon the little bit of oil left in the pan over them. Garnish with the reserved dill and parsley and serve at room temperature with wedges of lemon to squeeze over them.

500 g/1 lb. 2 oz. baby red, yellow
and orange (bell) peppers

2–3 tablespoons olive oil

300 g/10½ oz. feta cheese, rinsed
and drained

1–2 teaspoons finely chopped dried
red chilli/chile, or paprika

2–3 teaspoons dried oregano

1 tablespoon runny honey

1–2 tablespoons pine nuts

a bunch of fresh basil leaves, to garnish

SERVES 4–6

Preheat the oven to 200°C (400°F) Gas 6.

Using a small sharp knife, cut the stalks off the (bell) peppers and take out the seeds. Rinse and drain the peppers and place them in a baking dish. Pour over 2 tablespoons of the oil and place them in the preheated oven for about 45 minutes, turning them over from time to time until they have softened and are beginning to buckle.

Meanwhile, crumble the feta into a bowl and fold in the rest of the olive oil with the chilli/chile and oregano.

Take the (bell) peppers out of the oven and let them cool a little, until you can handle them. Using your fingers, carefully stuff the feta mixture into each pepper. Be careful not to overstuff them as the skin will split. Lightly squeeze the tips of the peppers together to prevent the feta from spilling out and pop them back into the preheated oven for 15 minutes.

Drizzle the honey over them and return them to the oven for 5–10 minutes.

Tip the pine nuts into a small pan and dry-roast them for 1–2 minutes. Sprinkle the roasted pine nuts on top and serve garnished with basil leaves.

Roasted baby peppers stuffed with feta

Stuffed peppers are perhaps the best known of the stuffed vegetables prepared for mezze. The most traditional are the small green ones stuffed with aromatic rice and served cold, or the larger (bell) peppers stuffed with minced/ground lamb and served hot. Here, brightly coloured baby peppers are stuffed with feta. Try a drizzle of honey over them to enhance the sweet and salty balance.

Red peppers stuffed with fennel

This colourful Italian vegetable dish is very easy to prepare and will wow your vegetarian friends. It can be made a day ahead and reheated.

4 tablespoons olive oil

4 fennel bulbs

4 large rectangular sweet red (bell) peppers

2 onions, finely chopped

3 garlic cloves, finely chopped

200 g/7 oz. ricotta cheese

80 g/³/₄ cup pistachio nuts, shelled and finely chopped

200 g/7 oz. passata/strained tomatoes

1 tablespoon tomato purée/paste

a handful of fresh flat-leaf parsley, finely chopped

a pinch of crushed dried chilli/chile (peperoncino)

fennel fronds, to garnish

sea salt and freshly ground black pepper

SERVES 3–4

Preheat the oven to 180°C (350°F) Gas 4. Grease a wide baking dish with 1 tablespoon of the olive oil.

Halve the fennel bulbs lengthways and trim them, discarding the woody cores and reserving the leafy fronds.

Blanch the bulb halves for 8 minutes in a saucepan of boiling water. Drain and pat dry. Halve the (bell) peppers lengthways and remove the pith and the seeds.

Heat 2 tablespoons of the olive oil in a frying pan/skillet. Sauté the onions and then add the garlic.

Transfer the onions and garlic to a large bowl and add the ricotta. Season with salt and pepper and add the pistachio

nuts. Place 3–4 spoonfuls of the mixture in each of the pepper halves. Place the fennel on top so that it sits on the cheese mixture. Add more mixture around the edges of each, to fill.

Transfer the peppers filled with cheese and fennel to the baking dish. Mix the passata/strained tomatoes and tomato purée/paste and season with parsley. Pour around the stuffed peppers. Drizzle the remaining oil on top of the peppers, and sprinkle with a pinch of dried chilli/chile peperoncino.

Cover with foil and bake for 30 minutes in the preheated oven until golden brown and bubbling. Serve garnished with fennel fronds.

Panzanella-stuffed tomatoes

The stuffed tomato is a classic Italian dish. This recipe is a version of an Italian tomato panzanella salad and benefits from a little cooking to release the flavours.

4 large or beef tomatoes

200 g/3¹/₂ cups cubed stale sourdough bread

1 small brown onion, sliced into thin wedges

2 celery sticks, sliced

1 garlic clove, crushed

1 cucumber, peeled, quartered and cut into small triangles

a small bunch of fresh basil leaves, finely chopped

2 tablespoons balsamic vinegar

50 g/²/₃ cup freshly grated Parmesan cheese

olive oil, for frying

sea salt and freshly ground black pepper, to season

mixed salad leaves/greens, to serve (optional)

SERVES 4

Slice a thin piece from the base of the tomatoes so they sit upright unaided. Slice about 1.5 cm/⁵/₈ in. from the top of the tomatoes, discard these slices or reserve to bake as a cook's treat. Carefully scoop out the tomato seeds and flesh and put in a bowl. Crush the seeds and flesh with the back of a fork to a coarse pulp.

Cover the base of a frying pan/skillet with olive oil and set over a medium heat. Once the oil sizzles when a cube of bread is dropped into the pan, add the rest of the bread and fry for 2–3 minutes, carefully tossing the bread cubes repeatedly to coat with oil and crisp up. Reduce the heat, then add the onion wedges, celery and crushed garlic and reduce the heat to cook over a low heat, tossing occasionally till the onions and celery have become translucent.

Preheat the oven to 180°C (350°F) Gas 4.

When ready to serve (no sooner or the bread will go soggy), mix the cooked ingredients with the tomato pulp, cucumber and basil. Season with a generous pinch of salt and the balsamic vinegar.

Stuff the tomatoes with the mixture and arrange on a baking sheet. Lightly cover with grated Parmesan and a little black pepper.

Bake in the preheated oven for 15 minutes and serve immediately as an appetizer or with mixed salad leaves for a main meal.

Provençal stuffed tomatoes

A satisfying classic French tomato dish, flavoured simply with fresh herbs, shallot and garlic. Serve as a light lunch or as a side to roast chicken.

Preheat the oven to 200°C (400°F) Gas 6.

Cutting across, slice a 'cap' off the top of each tomato, so as to reveal the seedy pulp inside. Using a small, sharp knife, carefully loosen the pulp from the tomato sides, then scrape out with a spoon, making four hollow tomato shells. Sprinkle inside the tomato shells with a little salt to draw out the juices, then turn upside down and set aside.

Heat the oil in a heavy-bottomed frying pan/skillet set over a low heat. Add the shallot and garlic and fry gently, stirring often, until softened, without allowing it to brown. Add the breadcrumbs, mix well and fry for 1–2 minutes. Remove the pan from the heat and stir in the thyme, chives, parsley and lemon zest. Season with salt and pepper.

Arrange the tomato shells in the prepared baking dish and fill them with the breadcrumb mixture. Top with the grated Parmesan cheese.

Bake in the preheated oven for 30 minutes until the Parmesan cheese is golden-brown. Serve hot or at room temperature.

4 large, firm-fleshed tomatoes, such as Coeur de Boeuf, Brandywine or other beefsteak tomato (each about 250 g/8 oz.)

sea salt and freshly ground black pepper

4 tablespoons olive oil

1 shallot, finely chopped

1 garlic clove, finely chopped

150 g/2¼ cups fresh breadcrumbs

1 teaspoon fresh thyme leaves

1 tablespoon freshly chopped chives

2 tablespoons freshly chopped flat-leaf parsley

grated zest of 1 lemon

2 tablespoons freshly grated Parmesan cheese

SERVES 4

Spelt stuffed squid

Squid bodies stuffed with risotto are a classic dish; this take on it uses spelt instead of rice to enable a tasty dish than can be stored in the fridge for several days ready to bake. The spelt holds its texture well, which preserves a firmness to the bite.

4 medium squid, cleaned

200 ml/³/₄ cup white wine

500 ml/2 cups Fish Stock (see page 62)

2 carrots, finely diced

2 celery sticks, finely diced

2 red onions, peeled and finely diced

300 g/2 cups pearled spelt

sea salt and freshly ground black pepper, to season

50 g/3¹/₂ tablespoons butter

2 red chillies/chiles

a small bunch of fresh flat-leaf parsley

50 g/³/₄ cup fresh grated Parmesan cheese

freshly ground black pepper

1 lemon, cut into wedges, to serve

SERVES 4

Prepare the squid following the instructions up to step 4 on page 23, then instead of opening out the head, clean and place a wooden spoon handle inside them. Cut three slices at an angle through one side of the body, using the spoon handle to stop you from cutting all of the way through the squid. Cut the legs into small pieces.

Pour the wine and stock into a saucepan set over a gentle heat. Add the carrots, celery and half of the onion and bring to a low simmer. Add the prepared squid to the pan and keep at a low simmer for 2 hours, topping up with a little water if it starts to reduce in volume.

Remove the squid bodies and set aside. Add the spelt and continue to simmer, taste the liquor and add a little salt if needed. The spelt will cook in 20 minutes, check it is soft to eat but retains a little bite. Drain and discard any excess liquid.

Stir in the remaining onion, the butter, chillies/chiles and parsley leaves. Save the parsley stalks and chop them finely, to garnish.

Stuff the reserved squid bodies with the spelt mixture and chill in the fridge – they can be kept refrigerated for several days like this.

Preheat the oven to 200°C (400°F) Gas 6.

Put the stuffed squid on a baking sheet and bake in the preheated oven for 15 minutes, the body should just be starting to colour and the spelt should be heated through. Remove from the oven, sprinkle with grated Parmesan and rest for 5 minutes while the Parmesan melts and the temperature of the spelt evens out.

Serve simply on a plate with a wedge of lemon, sprinkled with the chopped parsley stems and a little black pepper. The spelt should spill out of the body and use some of the reserved, cooked chopped legs to decorate the plate.

Savoy cabbage ratatouille parcels

These parcels have been designed to look extraordinary. By taking care to cook each element separately and then combine them in the parcels, the flavours of each ingredient is enhanced.

4 large leaves of Savoy cabbage

1 aubergine/eggplant, sliced into 1-cm/¹/₂-in. rounds

2 red onions, finely diced

1 onion, finely diced

1 red (bell) pepper, deseeded and finely diced

1 yellow (bell) pepper, deseeded and finely diced

1 courgette/zucchini, finely diced

olive oil, for frying

table salt, to season

a small bunch of fresh marjoram, to serve

TOMATO SAUCE

2 garlic cloves

1 teaspoon capers

400 g/2 cups canned chopped tomatoes

1 teaspoon white sugar

olive oil, for frying

SERVES 4

Preheat the oven to 160°C (325°F) Gas 3.

To make the tomato sauce, pour enough olive oil to coat the bottom of a small saucepan and add the garlic and capers. Set over a low heat to cook the garlic and capers until they are just starting to turn golden brown. Add the canned tomatoes and sugar, and leave to simmer on low for 10 minutes.

Using a handheld electric blender, purée the mixture to a smooth consistency and season with a pinch or two of table salt. Pour the mixture through a fine mesh sieve/strainer into a saucepan and set aside.

Put the Savoy cabbage leaves in a pan of boiling salted water and blanch for 2 minutes, then remove and pat dry with paper towels.

Preheat a frying pan/skillet over a high heat. Drizzle a little oil over the aubergine/eggplant slices, then carefully place them into the very hot pan/skillet and cook until they're just starting to blacken. Repeat on the other side, then remove

from the heat and allow to cool. Chop and dice the slices into about 5-mm/¼-in. pieces.

Add a light covering of oil to a frying pan/skillet. Set over a low heat and add the onions and (bell) peppers. Cover with a generous pinch of salt and leave to cook gently until the onions are translucent – this may take about 3–5 minutes. Add the courgette/zucchini and cook for another couple of minutes stirring gently. Remove from the heat, add the aubergine/eggplant pieces and gently stir to make the ratatouille.

Place the Savoy cabbage leaves into large ramekins, allowing the edges of the leaves to hang over the sides. Fill with the ratatouille mixture and fold the edges over to seal. Cover the top with foil to hold everything together.

Bake the parcels in the preheated oven for 20 minutes. Gently heat the saucepan of tomato sauce at the same time. Once cooked, carefully remove the foil and turn the parcels out onto large soup plates. Spoon the tomato sauce around the edge.

Decorate with fresh marjoram flowers and leaves and serve.

Brush or sprinkle the pita breads all over with the water and oil and either grill or bake in a preheated oven at 180°C (350°F) Gas 4 for 3–5 minutes or long enough to soften the bread, but not dry it. Cut off a strip from the long side, then pull open and part the sides of the breads to make a pocket. Push the strip inside. Keep the breads warm.

Put the oregano, lemon juice, grated onion and olive oil in a bowl and mash with a fork. Add the cubed meat and toss well. Cover and let marinate for 10–20 minutes. Drain, then thread the meat onto metal skewers. Cook on a preheated barbecue or stove-top grill pan for 5–8 minutes, or until golden outside and cooked through.

Put your choice of salad ingredients in a bowl, toss gently, then insert into the pockets of the pitta breads.

To make the dressing, put the yoghurt in a bowl, then beat in the garlic, cucumber and salt. Add a large spoonful to each pocket.

Remove the hot, cooked meat from the skewers, then push it into the pockets. Serve immediately, while the meat and bread are hot and the salad cool.

Note
Alternatively, you can roll the warm flatbread around the filling in a cone shape – a more common method in Greece. Unusually, they sometimes add fries to the cone, before wrapping in greaseproof paper.

Souvlaki in pitta

Souvlaki is the Greek equivalent of the kebab/kabob, a street food traditionally eaten at festival time. These days, it is mostly made of pork (though lamb is used when in season). Loved by locals and travellers alike, it is inexpensive, filling and delicious, with its pungent yoghurt, garlic and cucumber dressing and hot, soft pitta bread. In Greece, the local bread is often briefly pan-fried; at home it is better to brush pitta bread with oil and water and bake briefly, or put it under the grill/ broiler until heated through. Although pitta bread comes from the Middle East, not Greece, it 'pockets' beautifully, making the perfect receptacle for a meat and salad snack.

4 large pitta breads

water and olive oil, to moisten the bread

2 teaspoons freshly chopped oregano, or 1 teaspoon dried oregano, crushed

2 tablespoons freshly squeezed lemon juice

1/2 onion, coarsely grated

2 tablespoons extra virgin olive oil

500 g/1 lb. lean pork or lamb (usually leg meat), cut into 2-cm/3/4-in. cubes

salad, such as lettuce or cabbage, finely sliced

cucumber, sliced

red (bell) pepper, sliced

tomatoes, cut into wedges

radishes, halved

red onion, sliced into rings

GARLIC DRESSING

100 ml/1/3 cup thick, strained Greek yoghurt

4 garlic cloves, chopped and crushed

5 cm/2 in. cucumber, coarsely grated, then squeezed dry

1/2 teaspoon sea salt

metal skewers

SERVES 4

Fougasse

Fougasse belongs to the same ancient family of breads as focaccie, the original hearth breads. In Provence, these flat, slashed 'ladder breads' (so called because of their shapes) are highly decorative and often flavoured with olives or herbs. Sweeter versions contain orange flower water and almonds and are associated with feast days. Add a little buckwheat, triticale or spelt flour to the dough and you get even more flavour.

4 tablespoons extra virgin olive oil, plus extra for baking

450 ml/2 cups lukewarm water

2 teaspoons honey or syrup (optional)

250 g/1²/3 cups malted wheatgrain flour (or 200 g/ 1¹/3 cups malted wheatgrain flour plus 50 g/¹/3 cup buckwheat, triticale or spelt flour)

500 g/3¹/3 cups strong white/ bread flour, plus extra for kneading

1 sachet dried/active dry yeast, 7 g/¹/4 oz.

2 teaspoons sea salt

warm water, for baking

TOPPINGS
your choice of:
sliced garlic
onion rings
black olives, cut into strips
orange zest, finely sliced
orange flower water

2 large baking sheets, greased

MAKES 4

Put the oil, water and honey in a measuring jug and stir to dissolve. Put the flour or flours, yeast and salt in a food processor. With the motor running, pour the liquid through the feed tube to form a dense dough. Stop, then repeat for 30 seconds more, to develop the gluten.

Transfer the dough to a large, oiled bowl, and cover with an oiled plastic bag. Leave in a warm place for at least 30 minutes or up to 2 hours until doubled in volume.

Punch down the risen dough, transfer to a well-floured work surface and knead for 5–8 minutes or until silky and smooth. Return to the bowl, cover as before and let rise again for 20 minutes or until doubled in size, then divide into 4. Squeeze, pat and knead each ball into an oval. Pat or roll out each oval on an oiled baking sheet, until it is 3 times its original size, and about 1 cm/½ in. thick. Repeat the process with the second fougasse.

Make 2 rows of diagonal slashes in the dough, then open up the slashes to make larger holes. Tug out at the ends and sides if you'd like to open up the dough even more.

Brush the two breads all over with olive oil, then sprinkle with warm water. Add your choice of garlic, onion, olives, orange zest or orange flower water.

Bake each fougasse towards the top of a preheated oven at 220°C (425°F) Gas 7 for 15–20 minutes or until risen, crusty, but still chewy. Repeat with the other 2 portions of dough.

Serve warm and eat with your fingers, pulling the bread into short lengths.

Roast garlic rosemary focaccia

Freshly made focaccia is always a treat, with roast garlic adding a wonderful savouriness and rosemary an appealing aromatic note. Serve on its own or with Italian charcuterie, such as Parma ham/prosciutto or mortadella, for a light meal.

Preheat the oven to 180°C (350°F) Gas 4.

Slice the top off the garlic head, to expose the cloves inside. Wrap in foil and bake in the preheated oven for 1 hour. Unwrap the foil and set the garlic head aside to cool. When cool, squeeze out the softened garlic from 6 of the cloves and chop.

Mix together the flour, yeast, salt and sugar. Gradually add in the water and 2 tablespoons of the oil, bringing the mixture together to form a sticky dough. Turn out onto a lightly floured surface and knead until smooth and elastic. Then work in the roast garlic and 2 tablespoons of the rosemary. Transfer to the prepared mixing bowl, cover with a clean damp kitchen cloth and set aside in a warm place to rise for 1 hour.

Break down the risen dough and shape into a large oval on the prepared baking sheet. Using your fingertips, press into the dough to make numerous small indentations. Spoon over 2 tablespoons of the oil, so that it fills the indents, and sprinkle over the remaining rosemary. Set aside to rest for 30 minutes.

Preheat the oven to 200°C (400°F) Gas 6.

Bake the focaccia in the preheated oven until golden brown. Spoon over the remaining oil and sprinkle with the sea salt flakes.

Serve warm from the oven or at room temperature.

1 head of garlic

500 g/3$\frac{1}{2}$ cups strong white bread flour, plus extra for dusting

1 teaspoon fast-action dried yeast

1 teaspoon sea salt

1 teaspoon sugar

300 ml/1$\frac{1}{4}$ cups hand-hot water

5 tablespoons extra virgin olive oil

3 tablespoons rosemary leaves, finely chopped

a pinch of sea salt flakes

a large mixing bowl, oiled

a baking sheet, greased

MAKES 1 LOAF; SERVES 6

Mortadella olive tapenade and rocket sandwich

Mortadella has a tough time sometimes because it bears an unfortunate resemblance to pork luncheon meat. That's where the comparison ends; it tastes so much better and has a lovely, pure flavour and texture. This is a simple sandwich recipe combining some rich, dark flavours.

Lightly toast the slices of bread (or use them untoasted, if you prefer).

Spread butter over the toasted bread, then spread the olive tapenade over 4 of the slices. Add the slices of mortadella (2 slices per sandwich) – it's soft to bite so you won't need to shred it. Add some rocket/arugula to each and then a drizzle of balsamic vinegar.

Top each with a second piece of toasted, buttered bread to make 4 sandwiches. Serve immediately.

8 slices fresh bread of your choice

butter (at room temperature), for spreading

4 tablespoons Olive Tapenade (see page 10)

8 slices mortadella

a large handful of rocket/arugula

balsamic vinegar, to drizzle

MAKES 4 SANDWICHES

Roasted figs with Parma ham, gorgonzola and honey

This recipe shows off a stunning pairing of fruit and cheese, the crispy Parma ham acting as a corset that holds the little bundle together. The secret is to find figs that have just become ripe. Too early and they taste of nothing, too late and they disintegrate in the oven. You can double the quantities (as pictured) for larger groups.

Preheat the oven to 200°C (400°F) Gas 6.

Cut a cross into the top of the figs, cutting until you're about half way down. Squeeze the base of the figs so that they open like flowers.

Stuff some Gorgonzola into each fig, and wrap each fig with slice of Parma ham/prosciutto around the middle. You can use a toothpick to hold it in place if necessary.

Arrange the figs on the prepared baking sheet, making sure they have plenty of space between them for the heat to circulate and allow the ham to crisp up (there's nothing worse than soggy, steamed Parma ham).

Drizzle honey liberally over the figs, making sure you get some in the cavity.

Roast in the oven for 6–8 minutes, until the Parma ham is crispy and the cheese has melted.

Serve two baked figs per person, spooning over a few drops of reduced balsamic vinaigrette and any leftover cooking juices.

4 black or green figs, (whichever you prefer)

125 g/4^1/2 oz. Gorgonzola cheese

4 thin slices Parma ham/prosciutto

1 tablespoon runny honey

reduced balsamic vinaigrette, to serve

a baking sheet, lined with baking parchment

SERVES 2 AS A STARTER/ APPETIZER

TUNA TARTARE

150 g/5 oz. fresh tuna loin, sashimi grade

1/2 shallot, very finely chopped

1/2 medium-ripe avocado, finely diced

1 tomato, seeds and pulp removed, diced

1/2 tablespoon freshly chopped coriander/
  cilantro leaves

1/2 teaspoon freshly chopped mint leaves

25 g/1 oz. diced cantaloupe melon
  (about 1/2 wedge)

1/2 red chilli/chile, finely chopped
  (optional)

grated zest of 1/4 lime

olive oil, for drizzling

sea salt and freshly ground black pepper

rocket/arugula, to serve

PAPRIKA CRISPS/CHIPS

1/2 teaspoon smoked paprika, hot or mild

2 tablespoons olive oil (use a little more
  or less, according to taste)

2 white pitta breads

sea salt

**SERVES 2 AS A
STARTER/APPETIZER**

Tuna and melon tartare with paprika crisps

A stunningly simple recipe that works brilliantly as a light appetizer, especially on a hot summer's day when you feel like something clean and fresh. The crisps/chips are a great way to turn boring pitta bread into something a little more lively. They're pretty versatile and work well with all sorts of pre-dinner nibbles. Try them dipped in hummus or topped with guacamole, smoked salmon and soured cream.

Preheat the oven to 220°C (425°F) Gas 7.

Start by making the paprika crisps/chips – you can make these a couple of hours in advance if you want, as they'll keep well. In a large bowl, mix the paprika with the olive oil and some salt. Cut the pitta bread into small triangles and toss them with the olive oil-paprika mixture until they are nicely coated. Put them on a baking sheet, making sure that you only have one layer, or they'll go soggy. Bake them in the oven until they have turned golden brown and lightly charred at the edges. It should take about 5 minutes, but keep an eye on them. Once cooked, take them out and lay them out on a wire rack to cool and crisp up.

For the tartare, cut the tuna into small cubes. Gently mix with all the remaining ingredients, taking care that the melon and avocado do not turn to mush. The aim is to have a well-combined mixture, with each of the components distinctly visible. Serve the tartare simply spooned onto some rocket/arugula, or shaped with a ring mould with crisps/chips to the side.

Begin by scalding the tomatoes. Pour boiling water over the ripe tomatoes in a small pan or pot set over a medium heat. Heat for 1 minute, then remove from the water and carefully peel off the skin using a sharp knife. Roughly chop, reserving the juices.

Blend together the chopped tomatoes with their juices, the chilli/chile, garlic, caraway seeds, vinegar and ground coriander to a paste.

Heat the olive oil in a small frying pan/skillet set over a medium heat. Add the paste and fry, stirring often, for 8–10 minutes, until it thickens and reduces. Season with salt and set aside to cool – you will use this harissa paste to coat the sardines later.

Prepare the tomato salad. Finely slice the tomatoes and the lemon. Arrange the slices in a serving dish, pour over a little extra virgin olive oil. Sprinkle with parsley and season with pepper.

Preheat the grill/broiler to a medium heat.

Cut slashes in the sides of each sardine. Place them on the prepared baking sheet and spread each with the cooled harissa paste on both sides, making sure it gets inside the slashes.

Grill/broil the sardines for 6–10 minutes, until cooked through. Serve at once with the tomato salad on the side.

Harissa sardines with tomato salad

A spicy harissa paste adds a pleasant piquant kick to tasty sardines.

This is a great dish for the barbecue, when the sun is out.

200 g/¹/₂ lb. tomatoes

1 red chilli/chile, deseeded and finely chopped

1 garlic clove, chopped

1 teaspoon caraway seeds

1 tablespoon red wine vinegar

1 teaspoon ground coriander

1 tablespoon olive oil

8 plump fresh sardines, gutted

a pinch of sea salt

TOMATO SALAD

300 g/10 oz. ripe tomatoes, ideally in assorted colours

1 lemon

extra virgin olive oil, to drizzle

freshly chopped flat-leaf parsley, to serve

freshly ground black pepper, to taste

a large baking sheet, greased

SERVES 4

Griddled tuna with garlic bean purée and gremolata

Gremolata – traditionally served with osso buco – also goes very well with fish. Here firm-textured tuna steaks contrast nicely with the soft bean purée, while gremolata adds a refreshing zip. A great dish to make for dinner parties.

First, make the gremolata. Crush the garlic cloves with a pinch of salt to a paste. Mix together with the lemon zest and parsley and set aside.

Drain the beans, reserving 4 tablespoons of the bean water. Heat 1 tablespoon of the olive oil in a heavy saucepan. Add the onion and garlic and fry gently, stirring, until softened. Add the drained butter beans and reserved bean water, mixing in. Cover and cook gently for 10 minutes, stirring now and then.

Mash into a purée, season with salt and pepper and keep warm until serving.

Preheat the grill pan until very hot. Coat the tuna steaks with the remaining olive oil and season with salt and pepper. Griddle the tuna steaks until cooked to taste (about 2–3 minutes per side), turning occasionally to ensure even cooking.

Spoon the gremolata over the griddled tuna steaks and serve on a bed of bean purée, spooning over a little extra virgin olive oil for flavour and moisture.

2 x 400-g/14-oz. cans of butter beans/ lima beans in water

2 tablespoons olive oil

1 onion, finely chopped

1 garlic clove, finely chopped

4 tuna steaks, each approx. 200 g/7 oz.

sea salt and freshly ground black pepper

extra virgin olive oil, to garnish

GREMOLATA

2 garlic cloves

pinch of sea salt

finely grated zest of 2 lemons

6 tablespoons finely chopped fresh parsley

ridged stove top grill pan

SERVES 4

Greek-style baked fish with tomatoes

Chopped tomatoes give a lovely lift to this simple, easy-to-cook Mediterranean fish dish. Serve with crushed new potatoes and steamed green vegetables.

600 g/20 oz. ripe tomatoes

4¹/₂ tablespoons olive oil

2 garlic cloves, finely chopped

100 ml/6 tablespoons dry white wine

4 tablespoons freshly chopped flat-leaf parsley, plus extra to garnish

4 white fish steaks (125–150 g/4–5 oz. each)

sea salt and freshly ground black pepper

a baking dish, greased

SERVES 4

Preheat the oven to 200°C (400°F) Gas 6.

Begin by scalding the tomatoes. Pour boiling water over the ripe tomatoes in a heatproof bowl. Set aside for 1 minute, then drain and carefully peel off the skin using a sharp knife. Halve the tomatoes across, scoop out the soft pulp and finely dice the tomato shells.

Heat ¹/₂ tablespoon of the oil in a small frying pan/skillet. Add the garlic and fry gently for 1–2 minutes, until softened.

In a bowl, mix together the diced tomato, fried garlic, remaining oil, white wine and parsley.

Season the fish steaks with salt and pepper and place in the prepared baking dish. Spoon the tomato mixture over the fish steaks, then bake in the preheated oven for 20–25 minutes, until the fish is cooked through.

Sprinkle with a little extra chopped parsley and serve at once.

Grilled trout fillets with sauce vierge

This uncooked tomato sauce, with its Mediterranean flavours, goes well with the delicate fish. Serve it accompanied by new potatoes for a simple yet elegant meal.

350 g/³/4 lb. ripe tomatoes

1 small shallot, finely chopped

2 tablespoons finely chopped fresh tarragon leaves

2 tablespoons finely chopped fresh flat-leaf parsley

2 tablespoons shredded fresh basil leaves

4 tablespoons extra virgin olive oil

1 tablespoon red wine vinegar

sea salt and freshly ground black pepper

4 trout fillets (125–150 g/ 4–5 oz. each)

butter, for grilling/broiling

a baking sheet, greased and lined with baking parchment

SERVES 4

First, prepare the sauce vierge. Begin by scalding the tomatoes. Pour boiling water over the ripe tomatoes in a heatproof bowl. Set aside for 1 minute, then drain and carefully peel off the skin using a sharp knife. Halve the tomatoes across, scoop out the soft pulp and finely dice the tomato shells.

Mix together the diced tomato, shallot, tarragon, parsley, basil, oil and red wine vinegar. Season with salt and pepper, then set aside for 15 minutes to allow the flavours to meld.

Preheat the grill/broiler to a medium heat.

Place the trout fillets on the prepared baking sheet, season with salt and pepper and dot with a little butter. Grill/broil for 5 minutes until cooked through.

Spoon the sauce vierge over each trout fillet and serve at once.

Tuna carpaccio with lemon parsley sauce

This delicious treatment of tuna can also be used with sea bass and swordfish. This dish is enjoyed in the town of Marsala in Sicily, where the fish is sweet.

Place the tuna on a plate. Whisk together the oil, lemon juice, salt, pepper, oregano and parsley until emulsified.

Pour the sauce over the tuna. Cover and refrigerate for 1–2 hours, turning once during that period.

Arrange the leaves on a platter, top with tuna and serve garnished with lemon slices.

400 g/14 oz. fresh tuna, cut into very thin slices

4 tablespoons extra virgin olive oil (not too fruity)

freshly squeezed juice of 2 lemons

sea salt and freshly ground black pepper

1 tablespoon freshly chopped oregano

2 tablespoons freshly chopped flat-leaf parsley

250 g/9 oz. rocket/arugula, spinach or chicory/endive (or a mixture of all three)

1 lemon, sliced, to garnish

SERVES 4

Mussels three ways

Mussels work well with most alcoholic drinks. Cider adds a lovely apple sweetness that works well with the mussels and samphire adds a wonderful light salty flavour; wine is the classic accompaniment and is best served simply with crusty bread; while ale is hearty and the extra garlic adds depth and body to the dish.

WITH CIDER AND SAMPHIRE

1 brown onion, finely chopped

1 tablespoon vegetable oil

1 garlic clove, finely chopped

1 kg/2^1/$_4$ lbs. mussels

300 ml/1^1/$_4$ cups cider

150 g/5^1/$_2$ oz. samphire

50 ml/3^1/$_2$ tablespoons double/heavy cream

SERVES 4

WITH WINE (MEUNIÈRE)

2 red onions, finely chopped

1 tablespoon vegetable oil

1 garlic clove, finely chopped

1 kg/2^1/$_4$ lbs. mussels

200 ml/^{3}/$_4$ cup white wine mixed with 100 ml/^{1}/$_3$ cup water

50 ml/3^1/$_2$ tablespoons double/heavy cream

SERVES 4

WITH ALE AND GARLIC

1 brown onion, finely chopped

1 tablespoon vegetable oil

3 garlic cloves, finely chopped

1 kg/2^1/$_4$ lbs. mussels

300 ml/1^1/$_4$ cups ale

50 ml/3^1/$_2$ tablespoons double/heavy cream

SERVES 4

For each recipe, in a large pan set over a gentle heat, sweat off the onion in the vegetable oil until translucent. Then add the garlic (the garlic will burn if you add it at the same time as the onion) and continue to cook gently for another couple of minutes.

Meanwhile, prepare the mussels by gently rinsing under cold water and removing any 'beards'. Use a table knife (or any blunt knife) to scrape any loose barnacles off the shells and grab the beard with it to pull it off.

For mussels with cider and samphire, remove any hard stalks from the samphire, then finely chop.

Put all of the mussels into a saucepan set over a high heat, add the alcohol and cover. Bring to the boil for 2–3 minutes until the mussels have opened – don't overboil or you'll have rubbery mussels.

Take off the heat, add the double/heavy cream and samphire (if using), stir and spoon the mussels into big bowls (there's going to be a little grit at the bottom of the pan, so don't serve the last spoonful of the sauce).

Serve with generous hunks of bread to mop-up the delicious juices.

Note

Like most seafood, mussels should have no aroma; if they smell overly fishy or of ammonia, don't eat them. Discard any mussels that will not close when tapped gently, before cooking, as well as those which do not open after cooking.

From the grill

Nothing beats chargrilled meat, fish and vegetables
cooked over hot coals and packed with flavours of
the Mediterranean for a real taste of summer. From
al fresco roasted meat feasts in rural Italy to
Middle Eastern skewered fish cooked over the grill,
there is a long tradition of barbecuing in the Med.

Rosemary skewered sausages

All hail the sausage! A sausage is synonymous with a barbecue but this recipe gives it a bit of a kick by infusing the flavours of fresh rosemary right into the heart of every sausage. Most important here is making sure you buy good sausages, so the flavours don't get lost in bucket loads of fat. Lastly make sure you have a baguette to hand to wrap around the sausage – and some decent mustard wouldn't go amiss either!

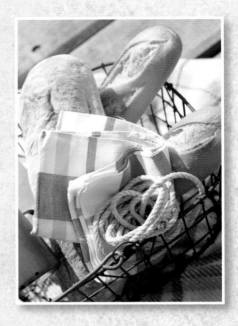

12 pork sausages of your choice

12 long sprigs of fresh rosemary

1 tablespoon olive oil

chunks of baguette, to serve

French mustard, to serve (optional)

a metal or wooden skewer

SERVES 6

Take a sausage and spear it lengthways with the skewer. Remove the skewer and slowly thread a rosemary branch through where the hole has been made. If the rosemary breaks do not worry, just thread the rest of the sprig into the sausage from the other side.

Repeat this process with the rest of the sausages and rosemary sprigs, then brush them with olive oil. Place the sausages on a hot barbecue/grill and cook for 10–15 minutes, turning occasionally to brown on all sides.

Serve the sausages in a torn baguette with some good French mustard, if liked, or simply hot off the barbecue.

680 g/1½ lb. lamb shoulder
1 lemon
6 fresh bay leaves

MINT AND LEMON THYME RUB
½ preserved lemon, finely chopped
1 tablespoon dried mint
2 tablespoons fresh lemon thyme leaves
60 ml/¼ cup extra virgin olive oil
freshly squeezed juice and grated zest
    of 1 lemon
sea salt and coarsely ground black pepper

6 x 30-cm/12-in. wooden skewers,
soaked in cold water before use,
or rosemary branches

MAKES 6 SKEWERS

To make the rub put all the ingredients
in a bowl and mix together. Season to
taste with salt and pepper.

Rinse the lamb under cold running water
and pat dry with a paper towel. Cut the
lamb into 3-cm/1¼-in. cubes and put
in a mixing bowl. Sprinkle the Mint and
Lemon Thyme Rub over the lamb and
toss to coat evenly. Season with black
pepper. (The salt from the preserved
lemon should be enough to season.)
Cover and refrigerate for 8–24 hours.

Slice the lemon in half, then cut each
half into half moons.

Remove the lamb from the fridge and,
while still cold, thread onto the prepared
skewers or rosemary branches, along
with the bay leaves and lemon slices.
Cover the skewers and allow to come
to room temperature.

On a medium–high barbecue/grill,
cook the lamb skewers for 5 minutes,
then reduce the heat to medium and
turn them over. Cook for a further 6–8
minutes, turning frequently to make sure
all the sides are brown and crispy. Serve.

Mint and lemon thyme lamb skewers

Chargrilled meats and pickles are always a good combo. Lamb shoulder holds up well on a hot grill and marinating overnight helps tenderize the meat. You could also use leg of lamb. If you have a lemon tree or rosemary bush in your garden, break off branches as these make excellent skewers.

Rack of lamb with harissa and pomegranate

Here, the spices of the harissa run wild with a hint of sweetness from the pomegranate molasses. Cut the lamb rack into double chops, grill them and serve.

HARISSA PASTE

2 dried black pasilla chillies/chiles or chilli/chile negro

1 dried ancho chilli/chile

2 red (bell) peppers

2 fresh red Serrano chillies/chiles

2 teaspoons caraway seeds

2 teaspoons ground cumin

2 tablespoons tomato purée/paste

1 teaspoon smoked paprika

1 garlic clove, roughly chopped

2 tablespoons extra virgin olive oil, plus a little to seal

sea salt and coarsely ground black pepper

a sterilized glass jar (see page 4)

RACK OF LAMB

2 whole racks of lamb

4 tablespoons Harissa Paste

1 tablespoon pomegranate molasses

seeds from 1 fresh pomegranate

SERVES 6

Put the dried chillies/chiles in 2 separate bowls and cover with boiling water. Allow to rehydrate for at least 2 hours, or up to 24 hours.

Over a high gas flame, blister the red (bell) peppers until the skins are black. Set aside and allow to cool, then peel off the skins and roughly chop.

Drain the rehydrated peppers, cut off the stems, and roughly chop.

Put the rehydrated chillies/chiles, (bell) peppers, Serrano chillies/chiles, caraway seeds, cumin, tomato purée/paste, paprika and garlic in a food processor and blend to a rough paste. Stir in the olive oil with a wooden spoon and season with salt and pepper.

Pour the harissa into a sterilized glass jar and pour a little more olive oil on top to seal.

Rinse the lamb under cold water and pat dry with a paper towel.

Cut the racks into double chops and place in a ceramic baking dish.

In a small bowl, mix together the Harissa Paste and pomegranate molasses and pour over the lamb. Rub into the meat, making sure it is well coated. Cover and refrigerate for 8–24 hours.

Remove the lamb from the fridge and stir to make sure all the sauce is on the meat. Allow the meat to come to room temperature.

Preheat a barbecue/grill to medium–high. Put the lamb, skin-side down, on the barbecue/grill and cook for 5 minutes, then flip over. Reduce the heat to medium and cook for another 6–8 minutes. Cook for longer if you prefer your lamb well done.

Plate the chops and sprinkle with the fresh pomegranate seeds.

Grilled lobsters with chive butter

Lobsters and Champagne is a special treat. First, boil the lobsters, then cut them in half and finish on the grill with lashings of flavoured butter and, of course, serve them with icy cold bubbly.

2 teaspoons sea salt

4 lobsters (about 680–900 g/
   1¹/₂–2 lbs. each)

sea salt and freshly ground black pepper

4 lemons, cut into quarters, to serve

CHIVE BLOSSOM BUTTER

1 bunch of chives with blossoms

225 g/2 sticks unsalted butterr,
   at room temperature

sea salt and coarsely ground black pepper

a large stock or pasta pot

SERVES 4

Separate the chive blossoms from the stems. Roughly chop the blossoms and finely chop the stems.

Put the chopped stems and butter in a food processor and process until smooth. Stir in the blossoms and season with salt and pepper. Refrigerate until ready to use.

Fill the stock pot three quarters full with water and add the salt. Bring to the boil and carefully add 2 of the lobsters. Cook for 10 minutes, then remove and place on a wooden chopping board. Cook the remaining 2 lobsters in the same way.

When the lobsters are cool enough to handle, cut them in half from head to tail using a sharp knife or scissors. Season well with salt and pepper.

Lay the lobster halves, cut side down, on a medium–high barbecue/grill and cook for 2–3 minutes. Turn them over and dot with the flavoured butters. Continue to cook for a further 3–4 minutes, until the butter has melted.

Serve immediately with more butter, lemons, and ice cold Champagne.

Asparagus with prosciutto

Fresh asparagus in season is pure delight. Add the delicate sweetness of Parma ham/prosciutto, dried to crispness, and you have an unusual combination. Use white asparagus if you can find it (French and Italian greengrocers often stock this during early summer), though green asparagus is more usual. Serve with a crisp, dry, white wine.

8 thin slices prosciutto, such as Parma ham, about 150–200 g/6–7 oz.

500 g/1 lb. bunch of thick asparagus

2 tablespoons extra virgin olive oil or lemon oil

a shallow baking sheet

SERVES 4

Before turning on the oven, hang the slices of prosciutto over the grids of the top oven rack. Slide the rack into the oven, then turn it on to 150°C (300°F) Gas 2. Leave for 20 minutes until the ham is dry and crisp. Remove carefully and set aside.

Using a vegetable peeler, peel 7 cm/3 in. of the tough skin off the end of each asparagus spear, then snap off and discard any tough ends. Arrange the asparagus in a shallow baking tray and sprinkle with the oil. Cook under a preheated grill for 6–8 minutes, or until the asparagus is wrinkled and tender.

Serve the asparagus with some of the hot oil from the grill pan and 2 prosciutto 'crisps' for each person.

Barbecued mackerel with tomatoes and onions

Barbecued mackerel is the taste of summer. This recipe is full of Mediterranean flavours and is easy to prepare in advance, ready to be placed on the barbecue and cooked. A little aniseed-flavoured Pernod thrown into the mix lifts this simple dish to something special.

8 medium tomatoes, each cut into 4 wedges

4 garlic cloves, thinly sliced

2 brown onions, roughly chopped

1 orange (bell) pepper, finely diced

50 ml/3½ tablespoons Pernod (or other aniseed-based liqueur)

sea salt and freshly ground black pepper

4 whole large mackerel (each about 170 g/6 oz.), cleaned and gutted

2 lemons, cut in half, to serve

SERVES 4

Begin by cutting four pieces of baking parchment about the same length as your fish and four pieces of foil a little larger than that. Place each piece of foil beneath the baking parchment and set aside.

Put the tomatoes, garlic, onions, and (bell) pepper with the Pernod in a large mixing bowl. Add a generous pinch of salt and pepper and mix together.

Place each fish on top of the pieces of baking parchment and foil, and cover with about a quarter of the tomato and onion mixture. Roll the paper and foil around the fish and seal by crimping the edges. Set in a fridge for a few hours to marinate.

When ready to cook, preheat a grill plate on the barbecue/grill before placing the mackerel packages on top. Cook with the lid closed for 5 minutes, then carefully open the packages and cook for a further 5 minutes with the lid open to reduce the amount of liquid in the packages.

Serve straight from the barbecue/grill, each with ½ lemon.

Tip

Barbecue/grill temperatures can vary so alter the cooking times to suit and check that the fish is fully cooked before serving. If you have smoking chips, add them for the final 5 minutes of cooking time with the lid closed to make a wonderful smoky, tomato sauce.

Barbecued octopus with grilled lemons

Octopus are delicious and dramatic to serve. This is a simple barbecue recipe that is best cooked outside as it is very smoky – the results are fun and a great talking point over conventional barbecue fare. Prepare the octopus and use the legs cleaned of any hard 'suckers'. Resist the temptation to cook the octopus for more than a couple of minutes or it will be like eating rubber, one minute on each side is plenty of cooking time.

Begin by making the marinade. Mix the juice and zest of 4 of the lemons with the yoghurt and spices in a mixing bowl. Coat the octopus legs with the marinade, cover and set in the fridge to chill overnight.

The next day, slice the remaining lemons into three slices each, sprinkle with a little sugar and set on the barbecue (or large ridged stove-top grill pan if cooking indoors) for 2–3 minutes until dark grill marks are formed. Turn the lemons over to cook the other side and add the octopus legs to the barbecue or pan. Turn the legs after 1 minute and cook the other side in the same way.

Serve the legs immediately with the grilled lemons – these can be squeezed over, or eaten with the legs.

8 lemons

250 ml/1 cup plain yoghurt

2 teaspoons coriander seeds

2 teaspoons ground cumin seeds

1 teaspoon ground turmeric

1 teaspoon allspice mix

2 teaspoons caster/granulated sugar

the legs of 1 large octopus (about 1 kg/2¼ lbs.), cleaned and portioned

SERVES 4

Chorizo and bean burger

No summer barbecue is complete without a beloved burger. Here the flavour combination of fresh minced/ground beef with a cured pork, like chorizo, works well.

BURGERS

400 g/14 oz. lean minced/ground beef

125 g/4¹/₂ oz. chorizo, finely diced

80 g/3¹/₄ oz. canned red kidney beans (drained weight), rinsed, drained and crushed

60 g/2¹/₄ oz. breadcrumbs

4 teaspoons tomato purée/paste

1 teaspoon freshly chopped parsley

sea salt and freshly ground black pepper

TO SERVE

4 crusty bread rolls or toasted English muffins, halved

salad leaves/greens

Caramelized Red Onions (see page 145)

SERVES 4 (MAKES 4 CHUNKY 175 G/6 OZ. BURGERS)

Put all the burger ingredients in a large bowl and mix together really well with your hands. Divide the mixture into 4 and then shape each portion into a burger.

To cook the burgers, fry them in a frying pan/skillet over medium heat for 12–15 minutes, turning a few times, until cooked through. Alternatively, pop them on the rack in a grill/broiler pan and cook under a preheated hot grill/broiler for 6 minutes on each side, until cooked through.

Serve the hot burgers in the bread rolls with some salad leaves/greens and the Caramelized Red Onions.

Grilled herb-stuffed pork skewers with bay leaves

This recipe hails from the San Domenico Palace Hotel in Taormina, Sicily – the chef, Massimo Mantarro, kindly jotted down the bones of this recipe.

Put the pancetta, garlic, egg, parsley, bread and salt in a bowl and mix well.

Gently beat the pork slices until uniformly thin. Spread each slice with a dollop of the pancetta mixture. Roll into cylinders and tie with kitchen string/twine.

Preheat a grill/broiler or barbecue/grill and coat the grill rack with oil. Thread each of the skewers with 2 pork bundles separated by bread squares and fresh bay leaves. Arrange the skewers on a baking sheet, drizzle with oil and season well with salt and pepper. Grill/broil over medium heat for 10–15 minutes, turning so that all sides are cooked evenly. Serve at once.

100 g/3½ oz. pancetta, smoked or unsmoked, diced

1 garlic clove, crushed

1 UK large/US extra large egg

2 tablespoons freshly chopped flat-leaf parsley

1 thick slice of country-style bread, soaked in warm water for 10 minutes and squeezed dry

750 g/1 lb. 10 oz pork loin, cut into 12 thin slices

6 x 5-cm/2-in. squares of country bread

approx. 36 fresh bay leaves

100 ml/7 tablespoons olive oil

sea salt and freshly ground black pepper

6 skewers

SERVES 4–6

Grilled tuna steaks with peperonata

4 tuna loin steaks cut 1 cm/½ in. thick

olive oil, for cooking

MARINADE

4 garlic cloves

3 tablespoons Dijon mustard

2 tablespoons grappa or brandy

sea salt and freshly ground black pepper

PEPERONATA

6 tablespoons olive oil

1 kg/2 lbs. fresh ripe tomatoes, skinned, deseeded and chopped, or 800 g/28 oz. canned chopped tomatoes

½ teaspoon dried chilli/hot red pepper flakes

2 medium onions, finely sliced

3 garlic cloves, chopped

3 large red (bell) peppers, halved, deseeded and cut into thin strips

sea salt and freshly ground black pepper

SERVES 4

Tuna is a very rich meat and is always cut thinly in Italy – never as thick as the seared steaks we are used to. Marinating the slices in mustard and grappa gives them a piquant crust – so good with the sweet peppers. Overcooking tuna can make it very dry, so watch it like a hawk.

To make the marinade, crush the garlic, put in a bowl and beat in the mustard and grappa. Season with salt and pepper and use to spread over the cut sides of the tuna. Arrange in a non-metal dish, cover and let marinate in a cool place for about 1 hour.

To make the peperonata, heat 3 tablespoons of the oil in a saucepan, then add the tomatoes and chilli flakes. Cook over medium heat for about 10 minutes until the tomatoes disintegrate.

Heat the remaining oil in a frying pan/skillet, add the onions, garlic and peppers and sauté for about 10 minutes until softening. Add the pepper mixture to the tomatoes and simmer, covered, for 45 minutes until very soft. Taste and season with salt and pepper.

Preheat the grill or barbecue. Sprinkle the steaks with olive oil and arrange on a rack over a foil-lined grill pan. Grill for about 2 minutes on each side until crusty on the outside and still pink in the middle. Alternatively, barbecue/grill over hot embers for slightly less time. Serve with the peperonata, which can be served hot or cold.

Devilled grilled chicken

Chicken and small game birds are very popular cooked this way. They are 'spatchcocked' – split open and flattened – so they cook evenly. The cooked spatchcocked bird is said to look like the shape of the devil's face (the legs being the horns), the charring is the colour of the devil and the chilli/chile makes it hotter than hell. The best way to eat these is with your fingers.

Turn the chicken breast side down. You will see the backbone underneath the skin, finishing with the parson's nose. Take a pair of kitchen scissors and cut along one side of the backbone. Cut along the other side and you will have removed the backbone completely. Turn the bird over, breast side up and open out. Press down hard on the breastbone until you hear a crack and the bird flattens out.

Put the olive oil in a bowl, add the lemon juice, garlic, chilli flakes, a good pinch of salt and lots of pepper. Mix well. Pour the mixture into a shallow dish, add the chicken and turn in the marinade to coat. Cover and leave to marinate in the refrigerator for at least 1 hour, or overnight.

Remove the chicken from the marinade and set it flat on one side of a mesh grill basket. Clamp the basket shut. Grill or barbecue bone side first for 20 minutes. Turn it over, lower the heat and cook for 20–30 minutes until cooked through and blackened but not burnt. Baste with the marinade from time to time. Serve hot with lemon wedges.

1 medium chicken

200 ml/1 cup olive oil

freshly squeezed juice of 1 lemon

2 garlic cloves, crushed

1 teaspoon dried chilli /hot red pepper flakes

sea salt and freshly ground black pepper

lemon wedges, to serve

a metal mesh grill basket

SERVES 4

Lamb and porcini kebabs/kabobs with sage and Parmesan

450 g/1 lb. tender lamb, from the leg or
    shoulder, cut into bite-sized pieces

2 tablespoons olive oil

freshly squeezed juice of 1–2 lemons

4–8 fresh medium-sized porcini, cut into
    quarters or thickly sliced

leaves from a bunch of fresh sage, finely
    chopped (reserve a few whole leaves)

2 garlic cloves, crushed

sea salt and freshly ground black pepper

TO SERVE

truffle oil, to drizzle

Parmesan cheese shavings

grilled or toasted sourdough bread

4 long, thin metal skewers

SERVES 4

Rural feasts in Italy often involve grilling and roasting outdoors. One of the most exciting times is the mushroom season when entire villages hunt for wild mushrooms and gather together to cook them. If you can't find fresh porcini, substitute them with dried porcini reconstituted in water, or field mushrooms.

Put the lamb pieces in a bowl and toss in half the oil and lemon juice. Add the sage and garlic and season with salt and pepper. Cover and leave to marinate for about 2 hours.

Thread the lamb onto skewers adding a quarter, or slice, of porcini every so often with a sage leaf. Brush with any of the marinade left in the bowl. Prepare a charcoal or conventional grill/broiler. Cook the kebabs for 3–4 minutes on each side.

Serve immediately with a drizzle of truffle oil and Parmesan shavings and toasted sourdough bread, if liked.

Lemon chicken kebabs/kabobs
wrapped in aubergine/eggplant

This Ottoman dish is impressive and tasty and best served with a refreshing salad, such as tomato and cucumber, or parsley, pepper and onion, and a buttery rice pilaf.

freshly squeezed juice of 2–3 lemons

2 garlic cloves, crushed

4–6 allspice berries, crushed

1 tablespoon crushed dried sage leaves

8 chicken thighs, boned and skinned

4 aubergines/eggplants

sunflower oil, for deep-frying

1 tablespoon butter

lemon wedges, to serve

4 metal or wooden skewers (optional)

an ovenproof dish, well greased

SERVES 4

In a shallow bowl, mix together the lemon juice, garlic, allspice berries and sage leaves. Toss the chicken thighs in the mixture, rolling them over in the juice, and leave to marinate for about 2 hours.

Peel the aubergines/eggplants in strips and slice them thinly lengthways, so that you have at least 16 long strips. Soak the strips in a bowl of cold, salted water for about 30 minutes. Drain them and squeeze out the excess water. In a wok or frying pan/skillet, heat sufficient oil for deep-frying and fry the aubergine/eggplant in batches, until golden brown. Drain on paper towels.

Preheat the oven to 180°C (350°F) Gas 4.

On a board or plate, lay two aubergine/eggplant strips, one over the other in a cross, then place a marinated chicken thigh in the middle. Pull the aubergine/eggplant strips over the thigh to form a neat parcel. Place the parcel, seam-side down, in the prepared ovenproof dish and repeat the process with the remaining thighs. Pour the rest of the marinade over the top and dab each parcel with butter. Cover the dish with foil and cook in the preheated oven for 30 minutes. Remove the foil, baste the chicken parcels with the cooking juices, and return to the oven for a further 10 minutes. Serve immediately, threaded onto skewers.

Vine-wrapped fish kebabs/kabobs
with tangy herb sauce

For these Mediterranean kebabs, almost any kind of firm, white fish fillet will do – monkfish or haddock work well. The fish is prepared in a simple marinade and then wrapped in the vine leaves, which become crisper with cooking.

about 30 preserved vine leaves

4–5 large, skinless fillets of white fish, with all bones removed

MARINADE

2–3 garlic cloves, crushed

1–2 teaspoons ground cumin

4 tablespoons olive oil

freshly squeezed juice of 1 lemon

1 teaspoon sea salt

TANGY HERB SAUCE

50 ml/ ¼ cup white wine vinegar or freshly squeezed lemon juice

1–2 tablespoons sugar

a pinch of saffron threads

1 onion, finely chopped

2 garlic cloves, finely chopped

2–3 spring onions/scallions, finely sliced

a thumb-sized piece of fresh ginger, grated

2 fresh hot red or green chillies/chiles, finely sliced

a small bunch of fresh coriander/cilantro, finely chopped

a small bunch of fresh mint, finely chopped

sea salt

a packet of short wooden or bamboo skewers, soaked in water before use

SERVES 4

First wash the vine leaves and soak them in several changes of water for 1 hour.

To prepare the marinade, mix all the ingredients together in a shallow bowl. Cut each fillet of fish into roughly 8 bite-sized pieces and coat in the marinade. Cover and chill in the refrigerator for 1 hour.

Meanwhile, prepare the tangy herb sauce. Put the vinegar in a small saucepan with the sugar and 1–2 tablespoons water. Heat until the sugar has dissolved. Bring to the boil for 1 minute, then leave to cool. Add the other ingredients, mix well and spoon it into small individual bowls.

Lay the prepared vine leaves on a flat surface and place a piece of marinated fish in the centre of each one. Fold the edges over the fish and wrap the leaf up into a small parcel. Push the parcels onto the individual skewers and brush with any remaining marinade.

Prepare a charcoal or conventional grill/broiler. Cook the kebabs for 2–3 minutes on each side. Serve immediately with a dish of tangy herb sauce on the side for dipping.

50 g/3¹/₂ tablespoons harissa paste

olive oil

600 g/21 oz. monkfish fillet, diced into
   2-cm/³/₄-in. pieces

8 red tomatoes, wedged

2 green (bell) peppers, diced into
   2-cm/³/₄-in. pieces

1 preserved lemon

150 ml/²/₃ cup vegetable stock

¹/₂ teaspoon ground cumin

¹/₂ teaspoon ground coriander seeds

¹/₂ teaspoon mild chilli/chile powder

100 g/²/₃ cup couscous

a small bunch of fresh coriander/cilantro,
   finely chopped

8 wooden skewers, soaked for
30 minutes

SERVES 4

Monkfish harissa kebabs/kabobs

A bit of fun and a taste of the southern Mediterranean. Harissa has chilli/chile, tomato and lemon flavours and these are reflected in these delightful kebabs/kabobs. Monkfish is a firm fish, ideally suited to stronger flavours.

Mix the harissa with a little oil until the mixture is loose and just liquid. Pat the monkfish with paper towels to ensure it is completely dry, then roll it in the harissa mixture to coat thoroughly.

Build the skewers with the monkfish, alternating pieces of tomato and (bell) pepper.

Peel the preserved lemon, reserving the peel. Carefully slice each segment ensuring there is no pith and set aside. Slice the peel into fine matchsticks and set aside.

Bring the stock to a simmer over a gentle heat, add the spices and a little oil, then the couscous. Stir the couscous to remove any lumps then cover and take off the heat, leaving it for 10 minutes to absorb the stock. Once the stock is fully absorbed, fluff the couscous with a fork and add a few pieces of preserved lemon peel to taste.

Set the skewers on a hot stovetop grill pan or a hot barbecue and cook, turning every minute or so until the pepper just starts to blacken. Serve on a bed of couscous and decorate with coriander/cilantro and lemon pieces.

Char-grilled prawns/shrimp

500 g/1 lb. 2 oz. fresh, large prawns/
shrimp, deveined and trimmed of
heads, feelers and legs

MARINADE

3 tablespoons tamarind pulp

250 ml/1 cup warm water

2 tablespoons sweet soy sauce

1 tablespoon sugar

freshly ground black pepper

TO SERVE

leaves from a small bunch of
fresh coriander/cilantro

2–4 fresh green chillies/chiles,
deseeded and sliced

a packet of wooden or bamboo
skewers, soaked in water before use

SERVES 2–4

*The aroma emanating from the
barbecue as the marinated prawns/
shrimp are grilled over charcoal will
make you feel very hungry.*

Rinse the prepared prawns/shrimp
well, pat dry and using a very sharp
knife, make an incision along the
curve of the tail. Set aside.

Put the tamarind pulp in a bowl and
add the warm water. Soak the pulp, until
soft, squeezing it with your fingers to
help dissolve it. Strain the liquid and
discard any fibre or seeds. In a bowl, mix
together the tamarind juice, soy sauce,
sugar and black pepper. Pour it over the
prawns/shrimp, rubbing it over the shells
and into the incision in the tails. Cover,
refrigerate and leave to marinate for
about 1 hour.

Insert a skewer into each marinated
prawn. Prepare a charcoal or conventional
grill/broiler. Cook the prawns/shrimp for
about 3 minutes on each side, until the
shells have turned orange, brushing
them with the marinade as they cook.
Serve garnished with the coriander/
cilantro leaves and chillies/chiles.

Swordfish kebabs/kabobs with oranges

Any firm-fleshed fish, such as tuna, trout, salmon, monkfish and sea bass, can be used for these mighty Middle Eastern kebabs. Make life easy and buy the swordfish ready boned from the fishmonger. Exotic sumac adds a lemony tang.

500 g/1 lb. 2 oz. boned swordfish, cut into bite-size chunks
2 oranges, cut into wedges
a handful of fresh bay leaves
2–3 teaspoons ground sumac

MARINADE
1 onion, grated
1–2 garlic cloves, crushed
freshly squeezed juice of ¹/₂ lemon
2–3 tablespoons olive oil
1–2 teaspoons tomato purée/paste
sea salt and freshly ground black pepper

4 metal skewers or 4–6 wooden skewers, soaked in water before use

SERVES 4

In a shallow bowl, mix together the ingredients for the marinade. Toss the chunks of swordfish in the marinade and set aside to marinate for 30 minutes.

Thread the marinated fish onto the skewers, alternating it with the orange segments and the occasional bay leaf. If there is any marinade left, brush it over the kebabs.

Prepare a charcoal or conventional grill/broiler. Cook the kebabs for 2–3 minutes on each side, until the fish is nicely browned. Sprinkle the kebabs with sumac and serve.

Note
Sumac is an increasingly popular spice. It grows wild, but is also cultivated in Italy, Sicily and throughout the Middle East. It is widely used in Lebanese, Syrian, Turkish and Iranian cooking. The red berries have an astringent quality, with a pleasing sour-fruit flavour. They are used whole, but ground sumac is available from Middle Eastern grocers or specialist online retailers.

2 aubergines/eggplants, cut into chunks

2 courgettes/zucchini, cut into chunks

2–3 (bell) peppers, stalks removed, deseeded and cut into chunks

12–16 cherry tomatoes

4 red onions, cut into quarters

MARINADE

4 tablespoons olive oil

freshly squeezed juice of $^1/_2$ a lemon

2 garlic cloves, crushed

1 teaspoon sea salt

PESTO

3–4 garlic cloves, roughly chopped

leaves from a large bunch of fresh basil (at least 30–40 leaves)

$^1/_2$ teaspoon sea salt

2–3 tablespoons pine nuts

extra virgin olive oil, as required

about 60 g/$^1/_4$ cup freshly grated Parmesan cheese

4–6 metal skewers or wooden skewers, soaked in water before use

SERVES 4–6

Summer vegetable kebabs/kabobs with pesto

Full of sunshine flavours, these kebabs can be served with couscous and a salad, or with pasta tossed in some of the pesto sauce. Home-made pesto is very personal – some people like it very garlicky, others prefer lots of basil or Parmesan – so simply adjust the quantities to suit your taste.

To make the pesto, use a mortar and pestle to pound the garlic with the basil leaves and salt – the salt will act as an abrasive and help to grind. (If you only have a small mortar and pestle, you may have to do this in batches.) Add the pine nuts and pound them to a paste. Slowly drizzle in some olive oil and bind with the grated Parmesan. Continue to pound and grind with the pestle, adding in enough oil to make a smooth sauce. Set aside.

Put all the prepared vegetables in a bowl. Mix together the olive oil, lemon juice, garlic and salt and pour it over the vegetables. Using your hands, toss the vegetables gently in the marinade, then thread them onto the skewers.

Prepare a charcoal or conventional grill/broiler. Cook the kebabs for 2–3 minutes on each side, until the vegetables are nicely browned. Serve with the pesto on the side for drizzling.

Char-grilled sardines in vine leaves with tomatoes

In all the markets along the eastern Mediterranean coast you will find stacks of fresh vine leaves, destined for dishes like this. If you are using fresh leaves, plunge them into boiling water for a couple of minutes to soften them then drain and refresh them before using them in the recipe. For vine leaves that are preserved in brine, soak them for 10–15 minutes in a bowl of boiling water to remove the salt, then drain, refresh and pat them dry.

DRESSING

4 tablespoons olive oil

freshly squeezed juice of 1 lemon

1 tablespoon balsamic or white wine vinegar

1–2 teaspoons of honey

1 red chilli/chile, seeded and finely chopped

a few fresh dill fronds, finely chopped

a few sprigs of fresh flat-leaf parsley, finely chopped

sea salt and freshly ground black pepper

8–12 fresh sardines, with the scales removed, gutted and thoroughly washed

2 tablespoons olive oil

freshly squeezed juice of ¹/₂ lemon

8–12 vine leaves, prepared as above

sea salt

olive oil, for brushing

4 fresh vine tomatoes, halved or quartered

SERVES 4

In a bowl, mix together all the ingredients for the dressing. Season to taste with salt and pepper and put aside.

Place the sardines in a flat dish. In a bowl, mix together the olive oil and lemon juice and brush it lightly over the sardines. Put aside for 15 minutes.

Meanwhile, prepare the charcoal barbecue/grill until just right for grilling. Spread the vine leaves on a flat surface and place a sardine on each leaf. Sprinkle each one with a little salt and wrap loosely in the leaf, like a cigar with the tail and head poking out. Brush each leaf with a little olive oil and place it seam-side down on a plate. Sprinkle the tomatoes with a little salt too. Transfer both the sardines and the tomatoes to the barbecue and cook on each side for 3–4 minutes, until the vine leaves are charred and the tomatoes are soft and slightly charred too.

Transfer the chargrilled sardines to a serving dish and arrange the tomatoes around them. Drizzle the dressing over the whole lot and serve immediately, while still hot.

Stuffed char-grilled sardines

This dish is best made with good-sized plump, fresh sardines, which are slit from head to tail with the back bone removed. Full of Mediterranean flavours, this is a great recipe for outdoor cooking on the barbecue while enjoying the summer sunshine.

To prepare the sardines, remove the bone, gently massage the area around it to loosen it. Using your fingers, carefully prise out the bone, snapping it off at each end, while keeping the fish intact. Rinse the fish and pat it dry before stuffing.

Heat the oil in a heavy-based pan and stir in the spring onions/scallions until soft. Add the garlic, cumin and sumac. Stir in the pine nuts and pre-soaked currants, and fry until the pine nuts begin to turn golden. Toss in the parsley and season with salt and pepper.

Leave to cool.

Place each sardine on a flat surface and spread the filling inside each one. Seal the fish by threading the skewers through the soft belly flaps.

Mix together the olive oil, lemon juice and sumac and brush some of it over the sardines. Prepare a charcoal or conventional grill/broiler. Cook the stuffed fish for 2–3 minutes on each side, basting them with the rest of the olive oil mixture. Serve immediately.

4 good-sized fresh sardines
2 tablespoons olive oil
4–6 spring onions/scallions, finely sliced
2–3 garlic cloves, crushed
1 teaspoon cumin seeds, crushed
1 teaspoon ground sumac
1 tablespoon pine nuts
1 tablespoon currants, soaked in warm water for 15 minutes and drained
a small bunch of fresh flat-leaf parsley, finely chopped
sea salt and freshly ground black pepper

FOR BASTING

3 tablespoons olive oil
freshly squeezed juice of 1 lemon
1–2 teaspoons ground sumac

a packet of wooden skewers, soaked in water before use

SERVES 4

To prepare these kebabs/kabobs successfully, you will need large metal skewers with wide, flat blades to hold the meat, which acts like a sheath to the sword.

KEBABS/KABOBS

500 g/1 lb. finely minced/ground lean
    lamb

1 onion, grated

2 teaspoons ground cumin

1 teaspoon ground coriander

1 teaspoon paprika

$^1/_2$–1 teaspoon cayenne pepper

1 teaspoon sea salt

a small bunch of fresh flat-leaf parsley,
    finely chopped

a small bunch of fresh coriander/cilantro,
    finely chopped

HOT HUMMUS

225 g/1$^1/_2$ cups dried chickpeas/garbanzo
    beans, soaked overnight and cooked
    in plenty of water until tender, or a
    410-g/14-oz. can cooked chickpeas/
    garbanzo beans, drained

50 ml/3 tablespoons olive oil

freshly squeezed juice of 1 lemon

1 teaspoon cumin seeds

2 tablespoons light tahini

4 tablespoons thick, strained
    natural yoghurt

sea salt and freshly ground black pepper

40 g/2$^1/_2$ tablespoons butter

TO SERVE

a leafy herb salad

flatbreads

2 metal skewers with wide, flat blades

SERVES 4–6

Cumin lamb kebabs/kabobs
with hot hummus

Mix the minced/ground lamb with the other ingredients and knead well.

Pound the meat to a smooth consistency in a large mortar and pestle, or whizz in a food processor. Leave to sit for an hour to let the flavours mingle.

Meanwhile, make the hummus. Preheat the oven to 200°C (400°F) Gas 6. In a food processor, whizz the chickpeas/garbanzo beans with the olive oil, lemon juice, cumin seeds, tahini and yoghurt. Season to taste, tip the mixture into an ovenproof dish, cover with foil and put in the preheated oven to warm through.

Wet your hands to make the meat mixture easier to handle. Mould portions of the mixture around the skewers, squeezing and flattening it, so it looks like the sheath to the sword.

Prepare a charcoal or conventional grill/broiler. Cook the kebabs/kabobs for 4–5 minutes on each side. Quickly melt the butter and pour it over the hummus. When the kebabs/kabobs are cooked on both sides, slip the meat off the skewers, cut into bite-sized pieces and serve with the hot hummus on the side with a leafy herb salad and flatbreads.

Al fresco feasts

These dishes have been designed to be prepared and served
with love at the finest of al fresco dinners or the most
modest of suppers. Packed full with the stunning flavours
and ingredients from the Med, you will find yourself
turning to these recipes all year around. All the well-known
feasts are here including the ubiquitous paella, hearty osso
buco and some inspiring pasta dishes to suit any guest.

Asparagus and prosciutto gratin

This is a delightful side dish to serve when asparagus is in season. It doesn't take much effort to put together and is always a crowd-pleaser.

12 asparagus spears

20 g/generous 1 tablespoon butter

150 ml/²/₃ cup crème fraîche/sour cream

1 teaspoon freshly chopped parsley

6 slices prosciutto

2 teaspoons breadcrumbs

2 teaspoons finely grated Parmesan cheese

sea salt and freshly ground black pepper

roasting pan, greased

SERVES 2

Bend each asparagus spear until it snaps, and discard the woody ends.

Steam the asparagus spears over a pan of boiling water for about 3–4 minutes, just to soften them – you don't want them fully cooked. Set aside.

Meanwhile, melt the butter in a frying pan/skillet and then stir in the crème fraîche/sour cream. Add the chopped parsley, season with salt and pepper, and remove from the heat.

Preheat the grill/broiler to medium.

Wrap a slice of prosciutto around 2 asparagus spears and lay them in the ovenproof roasting dish. Repeat with the remaining prosciutto slices and asparagus spears, laying them side by side in the dish.

Pour the melted butter and crème fraîche/sour cream mixture evenly over the top. Mix the breadcrumbs and Parmesan cheese together in a bowl and then sprinkle this over the top.

Grill/broil for 6–8 minutes, until nicely browned on top, then serve immediately.

Stewed fennel with olive oil, lemon and chilli/chile

The fennel absorbs all the flavours of the olive oil, lemon juice and chilli/chile and the anchovy adds a salty touch. Braising the fennel slowly makes it meltingly soft and tender with a hint of aniseed. This is delicious with pork dishes and more robust fish like swordfish. You can make this in advance and it only improves with keeping.

4 medium heads of fennel

200 ml/1 cup extra virgin olive oil

finely grated zest and juice of 1 large lemon

1 anchovy in oil or salt, rinsed and finely chopped

¹/₂ teaspoon dried chilli/hot red pepper flakes

a little white wine vinegar (optional)

sea salt and freshly ground black pepper

SERVES 4–6

Preheat the oven to 160°C (325°F) Gas 3.

Trim the stalks and fronds from the fennel. Discard the stalks, but keep the green fronds. Halve the fennel bulbs. Cut out the hard core, then cut each half into 2 wedges. Arrange in a flameproof baking dish.

Put the olive oil, lemon zest and juice, anchovy, chilli/red pepper flakes, vinegar, if using, salt and pepper in a bowl and whisk well. Pour over the fennel. Bring the dish to the boil on top of the stove. Cover with kitchen foil and bake in the preheated oven for 1 hour or until very soft and tender.

Remove from the oven and remove the foil. Taste the liquid and add a dash of vinegar to sharpen it if necessary. Serve warm or cold, sprinkled with the reserved fennel fronds.

This is better the next day after the flavours have matured.

2 tablespoons olive oil

2 shallots, finely chopped

1 celery stick, finely chopped

2 garlic cloves, chopped

2 bay leaves

5 sprigs of fresh thyme

$^1/_2$ teaspoon fennel seeds

50 ml/3$^1/_2$ tablespoons Pernod or dry white wine

400-g/14-oz. can of chopped tomatoes

50 ml/3$^1/_2$ tablespoons freshly squeezed orange juice

1 teaspoon grated orange zest

a pinch of saffron strands, finely ground and soaked in 1 tablespoon hot water

a pinch of Turkish chilli/ Aleppo hot pepper flakes

500 ml/2 cups fish stock

a handful of freshly chopped parsley, plus extra to garnish

500 g/1 lb. 2 oz. fish fillet, skinned and chopped into chunks

200 g/7 oz. raw prawns/ shrimp, peeled and heads removed, deveined

150 g/5$^1/_2$ oz. squid rings

sea salt and freshly ground black pepper

freshly chopped parsley, to garnish

a deep sauté pan

SERVES 4

Mediterranean garlicky fish stew

An appealingly colourful dish, perfect for a hot summer's day and ideal for entertaining. Serve with slices of baguette to soak up the fragrant broth.

Heat the olive oil in the deep sauté pan. Add the shallots and fry gently, stirring often, until softened and lightly browned. Add the celery, garlic, bay leaves, thyme and fennel seeds and fry, stirring, for 2 minutes until fragrant.

Pour in the Pernod or white wine and fry, stirring, until largely reduced. Mix in the chopped tomatoes and cook, stirring often, until thickened and reduced. Stir in the orange juice and zest, saffron soaking water and chilli/hot pepper flakes. Add the fish stock. Taste and season with salt and pepper accordingly. Mix in the parsley.

Bring to the boil and cook for 5 minutes. Add in the fish, prawns and squid rings and simmer until just cooked through – this takes just a matter of minutes. Garnish with parsley and serve at once.

Mushroom stew with walnut gremolata on soft polenta

Osso buco, a classic Italian meat dish, is the unlikely inspiration for this rich vegetarian stew. It's so packed full of flavour you won't notice there isn't any meat involved.

150 g/5 cups dried porcini mushrooms

5 fresh tomatoes

2 tablespoons olive oil, plus extra for frying

1 large onion, diced

1 tablespoon plain/all-purpose flour

150 ml/²/₃ cup white wine

700 g/1 lb. 9 oz. (about 6 caps) Portobello mushrooms, thickly sliced

350 g/5 cups button mushrooms, whole if very small or halved

200 g/3 cups oyster mushrooms, cut in half lengthways

2 teaspoons fresh thyme leaves

1 teaspoon dried chilli/hot red pepper flakes

1 tablespoon tomato purée/paste

sea salt and freshly ground black pepper, to season

WALNUT GREMOLATA

50 g/¹/₂ cup walnuts

25 g/¹/₂ cup freshly chopped flat-leaf parsley

1 garlic clove, crushed

grated zest of 1 lemon

SOFT POLENTA

200 g/1¹/₃ cups instant polenta/cornmeal

80 g/5 tablespoons butter

100 g/¹/₂ cup finely grated Parmesan cheese

1 teaspoon sea salt

SERVES 6

First make the gremolata. Put the walnuts on a baking sheet and roast in the oven at 170°C (325°F) Gas 3 for 5 minutes. When cool, chop finely, put in a small bowl and combine with the remaining ingredients. Season to taste and set aside until needed.

Put the porcini in a heatproof bowl and add 500 ml/2 cups boiling water. Set aside to soak.

Score the base of the tomatoes, put them in a heatproof bowl and add enough boiling water to cover. After 10 minutes remove them from the water, let cool then peel, deseed and chop the flesh. Set aside.

Heat 2 tablespoons of oil in a frying pan/skillet set over a medium heat. Add the onion and cook, stirring, for about 10 minutes, until the onion has softened but not coloured. Increase the heat and add the flour. Stir to incorporate and cook for 1 minute. Add the wine and let it bubble for 1 minute, deglazing the pan with a wooden spoon. Remove from the heat and set aside.

Heat 1 tablespoon of oil in a large frying pan/skillet set over a medium–high heat. Add the Portobello and button mushrooms in batches and fry until lightly brown, adding more oil between batches as necessary. Remove the pan from the heat while you drain the porcini and squeeze out excess liquid (reserving the soaking water for later).

Chop the porcini and add them to the other mushrooms in the pan, along with the oyster mushrooms. Add the reserved onion mixture, thyme, chilli/hot pepper flakes, tomato purée/paste, chopped fresh tomatoes and 375 ml/1¹/₂ cups of the reserved porcini soaking liquid. Return the pan to the heat and simmer gently for 20 minutes, until the sauce has thickened. Season to taste with salt and pepper.

To make the polenta, bring 1 litre/4 cups water to the boil in a medium saucepan and add the salt.

Pour in the polenta and stir constantly over a very gentle heat for about 10 minutes, until the polenta is coming away from the sides and is smooth in texture – watch out as it will splatter.

Add the butter and Parmesan, beat well to combine, taste and adjust the seasoning as required.

Pour the polenta into a serving dish, ladle on the mushroom stew and sprinkle with the Walnut Gremolata. Serve immediately.

Osso buco with orange gremolata

Osso buco, or 'cross-cut veal shank', is a cheap, hearty and easy to cook meat that is often underused. It's suitable for all sorts of slow-cooked dishes. This is a relatively traditional recipe and a good introduction to the meat, but don't stop at this — experiment with it.

Season the flour with a little salt and pepper, then toss your osso buco in it, making sure they are nicely coated.

Heat a heavy-based pan or casserole dish over high heat. Add a splash of vegetable oil and fry the osso buco for about 3 minutes each side, until nicely browned all over. Don't overcrowd the pan; you want to caramelize the outside of the meat, not steam it.

Remove the osso buco and set aside. Empty out the pan and give it a quick wash if there are any burnt bits stuck to it. Heat it up again over medium heat and add the olive oil, onion, garlic, carrot, celery and fennel. Cook for about 10 minutes, or until the onions are beginning to brown.

Add the red wine, rosemary and bay leaf. Bring to the boil and allow to simmer away until reduced by half. Add the tomatoes, osso buco and half the beef stock/broth. Bring to a simmer, then reduce the heat to its lowest setting and simmer for 1½–2 hours. Add a little more beef stock/broth if the sauce seems to be thickening too much as it cooks. You want the meat to be meltingly soft, but still just attached to the bone.

Prepare the orange gremolata by mixing together all the ingredients and loosening it with a little olive oil.

Serve the osso buco on a bed of creamy mashed Désirée potatoes or polenta, with the gremolata spooned on top.

OSSO BUCO
flour, for dusting

2 x osso buco (cross-cut veal shanks), about 300 g/11 oz. each

vegetable oil, for frying

100 ml/¹/₃ cup olive oil

1 small white onion, chopped

1 garlic clove, chopped

1 small carrot, chopped

1 celery stick, thinly sliced

½ small bulb fennel, chopped

100 ml/¹/₃ cup red wine

1 sprig fresh rosemary

1 bay leaf

400 g/14 oz. canned chopped tomatoes

about 250 ml/1 cup beef stock/broth

sea salt and freshly ground black pepper

mashed Désirée potatoes or polenta, to serve

ORANGE GREMOLATA
grated zest of ½ orange and ½ lemon

a small bunch of flat-leaf parsley, roughly chopped

½ garlic clove, finely chopped

SERVES 2

Provençal beef daube with lemon and parsley

A Provençal daube of beef is a grand, classic stew, left bubbling for hours, enriched with a slice of pork or bacon rind, and fragrant with red wine. This is a simplified version, so there's time to make the aromatic lemon, parsley and garlic gremolata topping (not Provençal but Italian). Traditionally, gremolata is served with the Italian dish osso buco, but it has been known to migrate west into French dishes – a familiar Mediterranean tendency.

1 kg/2¼ lbs. beef topside or beef round steak, cut 3 cm/1 in. thick

2 tablespoons extra virgin olive oil

10 garlic cloves, sliced

250 g/8 oz. unsmoked (slab) bacon, cubed

2 red onions, quartered

4 medium carrots, left whole

6 plum tomatoes, cut into wedges

zest of 1 lemon removed with a lemon zester

1 fresh bouquet garni of thyme, bay, parsley and oregano, tied with twine

75 g/3 oz. prunes, preferably Agen type

250 ml/1 cup rich red wine, such as Cahors

200 ml/ ¾ cup boiling beef stock

a bunch of flat-leaf parsley, freshly chopped

2 tablespoons fresh brioche or breadcrumbs (optional)

sea salt and freshly ground black pepper

SERVES 4

Beat the beef all over with a meat hammer or rolling pin, then cut it into 5-cm/2-in. square chunks. Heat the oil in a large, flameproof casserole, add the beef, in batches if necessary, and sauté for 4 minutes on each side. Remove with a slotted spoon and set aside.

Add 2 of the garlic cloves to the pan, then add the bacon, onions and carrots.

Stir and sauté until the bacon is golden and the fat has run. Add the tomatoes, half the lemon zest, the bouquet garni, prunes, wine and stock. Replace the browned beef, pushing the pieces well down under the liquid.

Remove and discard the white pith from the lemon. Cut the flesh into tiny cubes and add to the pan.

Reduce the heat to a gentle simmer. Cover with a lid and cook, undisturbed, for 1½ hours, then test for doneness.

(If preferred, cook in a low oven at 150°C (300°F) Gas 2 for 2½ hours or until tender.)

To make the gremolata, chop the remaining garlic, and mix with the remaining lemon zest, the parsley and breadcrumbs.

Serve the daube with a little of its sauce and the gremolata sprinkled on top.

Like most stews, the daube will improve over several days. Serve the rest at a later meal, perhaps with mashed potatoes.

1 tablespoon olive oil

4 shallots, finely chopped

1 garlic clove, finely chopped

100 g/3³/4 oz. skinless, boneless chicken breast or thigh meat, diced

100 g/3³/4 oz. chorizo, diced

100 g/3³/4 oz. pancetta, diced

1 red (bell) pepper, deseeded and roughly chopped

a small handful of green beans, trimmed and roughly chopped

200 g/7 oz. shelled uncooked seafood (such as scallops, mussels and sliced squid)

12–14 uncooked king prawns/jumbo shrimp, shelled and deveined

1 small fresh red chilli/chile, deseeded and finely chopped

1 teaspoon sweet smoked Spanish paprika

a pinch of chipotle powder (optional)

50 g/¹/2 cup frozen or fresh peas

a small handful of freshly chopped parsley

a pinch of freshly chopped or dried thyme

6 tablespoons white wine (preferably dry)

500 ml/generous 2 cups hot chicken stock

150 g/5 oz. paella rice, such as Bomba

a small pinch of saffron strands

sea salt and freshly ground black pepper

crème fraîche/sour cream and 1 lemon, quartered, to serve (optional)

SERVES 2

Paella

Paella is so simple, so delicious and it's a great way to whisk your guests away to sunnier climes. This is Mediterranean comfort food at its best.

Put the olive oil in a frying pan/skillet over medium heat and get it nice and hot, then add the shallots and garlic and cook them until browned. Then, it's a simple process of adding everything as you go through the list. Add the chicken and cook, turning regularly, until sealed. Add the chorizo and stir for 20 seconds, then add the pancetta and cook, stirring, until the pancetta and chorizo are becoming crisp. Add the red (bell) pepper, and stir for 20 seconds, then add the green beans and cook for 20 seconds. Add the seafood and prawns/shrimp, followed by the chilli/chile and spices, and stir to coat everything. Add the peas and herbs, then add the wine and turn the heat up to bubble the wine for 2 minutes. Add the stock, rice and saffron, then season with salt and pepper.

Turn the heat right down so the mixture is just lightly bubbling and cook, stirring occasionally, for 15–20 minutes, until the rice has absorbed all the liquid and all the ingredients are cooked. You'll know if you like it a bit runny, or thicker, so just keep an eye on the consistency and be sure to taste the rice towards the end of cooking so that you know it is definitely cooked. You can always add a little more hot stock if you want the rice 'fluffier' and then just cook for a bit longer.

Once the paella is ready, serve it immediately with the crème fraîche/sour cream and lemon quarters.

Soft polenta with sausage ragù

Polenta is the staple carbohydrate in the north of Italy. In some mountain trattorias polenta is poured straight onto a huge wooden board set in the middle of the table. The sauce is then poured into a large hollow in the centre of the polenta and diners helps themselves directly from the pile.

To make the ragù, squeeze the sausage meat out of the skins into a bowl and break up the meat. Heat the oil in a medium saucepan and add the onion. Cook for 5 minutes until soft and golden. Stir in the sausage meat, browning it all over and breaking up the lumps with a wooden spoon. Pour in the passata and the wine. Bring to the boil. Add the sun-dried tomatoes. Simmer for 30 minutes or until well reduced, stirring occasionally. Add salt and pepper to taste.

Meanwhile, bring 1.4 litres/6 cups water to the boil with 2 teaspoons salt. Sprinkle in the polenta, stirring or whisking to prevent lumps forming.

Simmer for 5–10 minutes, stirring constantly, until thickened like soft mashed potato. Quickly spoon the polenta into 4 large, warm soup plates and make a hollow in the centre of each. Top with the sausage ragù and serve with grated Parmesan cheese.

2 teaspoons sea salt

300 g/2 cups instant polenta/cornmeal

*freshly grated Parmesan cheese,
   to serve*

SAUSAGE RAGÙ

*500 g/1 lb. fresh Italian pork sausages
   or good all-meat pork sausages*

2 tablespoons olive oil

1 medium onion, finely chopped

*500 ml/2 cups tomato passata
   (strained crushed tomatoes)*

150 ml/²/₃ cup dry red wine

*6 sun-dried tomatoes in oil,
   drained and sliced*

*sea salt and freshly ground
   black pepper*

SERVES 4

Polenta puttanesca

A feisty, spicy Italian tomato sauce contrasts nicely with the comforting blandness of grilled polenta in this hearty dish.

200 g/1⅓ cups instant polenta/cornmeal

2 tablespoons olive oil

1 garlic clove, peeled and chopped

6 anchovy fillets in oil, chopped

800 g/1¾ lbs. canned peeled cherry tomatoes

2 small dried chillies/chiles, finely chopped

2 teaspoons capers, rinsed

2 generous pinches of dried oregano

freshly ground black pepper

freshly chopped flat-leaf parsley, to garnish

a 23-cm/9-in. square baking pan, greased

SERVES 4

First, prepare the polenta. Put the polenta and 800 ml/3⅓ cups of cold water in a large saucepan or pot and season well with salt. Set over a medium–high heat and bring to the boil, stirring continuously. Reduce the heat and simmer, stirring often, until the polenta thickens and begins to come away from the sides of the pan. Transfer to the prepared baking pan, patting smooth with the back of a spoon and set aside to cool.

While the polenta is cooling, prepare the puttanesca sauce. Heat the olive oil in large frying pan/skillet set over a medium heat.

Add the garlic and fry until fragrant. Then add the anchovy fillets and fry until they melt in the pan. Mix in the cherry tomatoes, dried chillies/chiles, capers and oregano and season with pepper. Cook, stirring often, for 15–20 minutes, until the sauce has reduced and thickened.

Preheat the oven to 110°C (225°F) Gas ¼.

Cut the cooled, set polenta into 8 even-sized squares.

Preheat an oiled, ridged stovetop grill pan until very hot, then cook the polenta in batches until marked by the griddle on each side, keeping each square warm in the preheated oven.

Gently heat through the puttanesca sauce over a low heat, then spoon over the grilled polenta squares and sprinkle over the parsely, to serve.

Caponata with grilled polenta and whipped feta

Caponata is one of those dishes that improves with age and is extremely versatile. Served here with baked polenta, it makes a great vegetarian lunch or appetizer. It is also delicious as an accompaniment to grilled fish or chicken.

700 g/7 cups (about 2) diced
   aubergine/ eggplant

125 ml/¹/₂ cup olive oil

1 large onion, diced

1 garlic clove, crushed

1 red plus 1 orange or yellow (bell)
   pepper, deseeded and diced

2 celery sticks, cut on an angle into
   2-cm/³/₄-in. slices

4 tablespoons red wine vinegar

400-g/14-oz. can chopped tomatoes

2 teaspoons caster/granulated sugar

35 g/¹/₃ cup green olives, pitted and halved

1 tablespoon capers, rinsed and drained

20 g/¹/₄ cup flaked/slivered almonds,
   lightly toasted

sea salt and freshly ground black pepper

a handful of fresh flat-leaf parsley, to
   serve

GRILLED POLENTA

200 g/1¹/₃ instant polenta/cornmeal

80 g/5 tablespoons butter

50 g/1 cup freshly grated Parmesan
   cheese

WHIPPED FETA

250 g/2 cups feta cheese

60 ml/¹/₄ cup Greek yoghurt

60 ml/¹/₄ cup extra virgin olive oil

1 tablespoon freshly squeezed lemon juice

an 18 x 25-cm/7 x 10-in. baking pan,
greased

a baking sheet, greased

SERVES 6

To make the caponata, place the aubergine/eggplant in a colander and sprinkle with salt. Leave for 30 minutes then rinse under cold, running water and pat dry with a paper towel.

Heat the oil in a large, heavy-bottomed saucepan or pot set over a medium heat. Add the aubergine/eggplant and fry for 5–8 minutes, until golden brown, stirring occasionally. Remove from the pan and set aside.

Add the onion to the same pan and fry for 5 minutes, or until softened. You may need to add a little more oil.

Add the garlic and cook for another minute before adding the peppers and celery. Cook for 5 minutes, then add the vinegar and stir to deglaze the pan.

Stir in the tomatoes and sugar and simmer for 5–10 minutes.

Return the aubergine/eggplant to the pan with the olives and capers, and mix well. Cook for a further 5 minutes. Remove from the heat, season and stir in the almonds.

To make the polenta, bring 1 litre/4 cups of salted water to the boil in a medium saucepan or pot. Gradually pour in the polenta while stirring continuously with a wooden spoon to prevent lumps forming. Reduce the heat and keep stirring for about 5 minutes. Remove from the heat and stir in the butter and the Parmesan. Taste and adjust the seasoning as necessary.

Working quickly, spread the polenta mix evenly across the prepared baking pan to a layer 2 cm/¾ in. deep. Set aside to cool.

To make the Whipped Feta, crumble the feta into a food processor and pulse together with the yoghurt until smooth. Add the oil and mix until it becomes very soft and spreadable. Add the lemon juice and set in the fridge.

Preheat a grill/broiler to a medium heat. Tip the set polenta onto a chopping board and cut into 6 rectangles. Then cut these in half diagonally to give you 12 triangles.

Place the polenta on the prepared baking sheet and set under the grill/broiler to cook for about 10 minutes, or until golden. Turn the polenta and grill the other side in the same way.

Reheat the caponata over a medium heat, add the chopped parsley and stir through. Heap the caponata onto a plate, top with the Grilled Polenta and a dollop of Whipped Feta. Sprinkle with pepper and serve with a green salad.

Orzo with roast courgettes/zucchini and tomato dressing

If the thought of pasta salad makes you recoil with images of cold pasta mixed with canned corn, drowned in mayo, fear not – this fresh, vibrant salad bears no resemblance.

Preheat the oven to 200°C (400°F) Gas 6.

Begin by making the dressing. Cut the top part off the top of the garlic head to expose the individual garlic cloves. Place the garlic head, cut-side down, onto a square piece of foil and drizzle with 2 teaspoons of olive oil. Lift the foil up around the garlic and place on a baking sheet. Roast in the preheated oven for 45 minutes. Remove from the oven, open the foil wrap and set aside to cool. When the garlic is cool enough to handle, squeeze the cloves out of the skin, coarsely chop the garlic flesh and discard the skin.

Reduce the oven temperature to 180°C (350°F) Gas 4.

Place 50 g/½ cup of the semi-dried tomatoes in a food processor with the remaining olive oil, sugar, vinegar, salt and pepper. Blend and pour into a large mixing bowl.

Roughly chop the remaining semi-dried tomatoes and stir through the oil mixture with the roasted garlic.

To prepare the orzo pasta, place it in a saucepan or pot of salted boiling water set over a medium heat. Bring to the boil and cook for about 8 minutes until al dente. Drain well before transferring to the bowl with the dressing while still warm. Toss to coat the orzo.

Preheat the stove-top grill-pan over a medium heat and, when hot, grill the courgettes/zucchini, flesh-side down for 2 minutes until marked. Transfer the courgettes/zucchini skin-side down to a baking sheet, season with salt and pepper and cook in the still-warm oven for 10 minutes. Remove from the oven and cut on the diagonal at 2-cm/¾-in. intervals.

Add the courgettes/zucchini, feta, olives and parsley and stir. Add a final drizzle of olive oil and serve.

250 g/4 cups orzo pasta

400 g/12 oz. (about 2) courgettes/zucchini, cut in half lengthways

70 g/²/₃ cup feta

70 g/²/₃ cup black olives, pitted and halved

20 g/scant ½ cup flat-leaf parsley, chopped

sea salt and freshly ground black pepper, to season, plus extra for the dressing

DRESSING

1 head of garlic

125 ml/½ cup olive oil, plus 2 teaspoons to roast

80 g/¾ cup semi-dried tomatoes in oil, drained

¼ teaspoon caster/granulated sugar

1 tablespoon balsamic vinegar

a ridged stove top grill pan

SERVES 6

Risotto with red wine, mushrooms and pancetta

Risotto made with red wine is a miracle of flavour combinations. The sweetness from the mushrooms and cheese and the smoky saltiness from the pancetta make this unforgettable. The important thing to remember is to reduce the wine completely to boil off the alcohol and reduce the acidity. This is a risotto to make in the colder months, when you need big, comforting flavours. Don't let the risotto overcook and become stodgy.

Heat half the oil or butter in a large saucepan and add the chopped pancetta, cook until the fat begins to run, then add the onion and mushrooms. Cook gently for 5 minutes until softened and translucent.

Stir in the rice and cook for 1–2 minutes until the rice smells toasty and looks opaque. Add the Chianti wine and boil hard until the liquid disappears.

Add a ladle of hot stock and simmer, stirring until absorbed. Continue adding the stock ladle by ladle until only 2 ladles of stock are left. The rice should be tender but still have some bite to it (this should take 15–18 minutes). As soon as the rice is tender, stir in the remaining olive oil and all the Parmesan. Taste and season well with salt and pepper.

Finally, stir in the remaining stock and let stand with the lid on for 5 minutes. Transfer to a large, warmed bowl and sprinkle with parsley. Top with the fried porcini, if using, and serve immediately.

4 tablespoons olive oil or 75 g/5 tablespoons unsalted butter

75 g/3 oz. pancetta, finely chopped

1 red onion, finely chopped

200 g/8 oz. large dark mushrooms or porcini, finely chopped

500 g/2^1/$_2$ cups Italian risotto rice, such as arborio

250 ml/1 cup good Chianti wine

about 1.5 litres/1^1/$_2$ quarts good-quality light chicken or meat stock, well heated

100 g/1 cup freshly grated Parmesan cheese

sea salt and freshly ground black pepper

TO SERVE

2 tablespoons freshly chopped flat-leaf parsley

1 porcini, sliced and pan-fried in olive oil until golden, to serve (optional)

SERVES 6

Mediterranean pasta bake with crispy baked salami

This is a good one for entertaining because you can prepare and throw everything together earlier in the day, then all you have to do is bake the dish and add the crispy salami in the last 10 minutes. It looks like more effort than it is as well.

To make the salami chips, preheat the oven to 180°C (350°F) Gas 4.

Lay the slices of salami in a single layer on a baking sheet. Bake in the preheated oven for 20–25 minutes, until crisp. Keep checking that they're not burning. Remove from the oven and leave to cool. Store in an airtight container in the refrigerator. These chips will last for up to a week in the refrigerator and are the perfect thing to nibble on.

For the pasta bake, heat the olive oil in a frying pan/skillet over medium heat until hot, then add the onion, garlic, courgette/zucchini, aubergine/eggplant, red (bell) pepper and mushrooms, and fry until they're all soft and browning. Add the tomato purée/paste and pesto, season with salt and pepper, and stir together for a minute, then add the canned tomatoes. Reduce the heat and simmer for 10 minutes.

Meanwhile, cook the pasta in a large pan of lightly salted boiling water for 3 minutes (it's only to soften it), then drain well and return to the pan. Add the vegetable mixture and stir well, then stir in the crème fraîche/sour cream. Taste and add more seasoning, if you like. Transfer the mixture to an ovenproof dish and spread evenly. At this point, you can cover the dish with foil and leave it for a while before baking, or cool it, then chill in the refrigerator for up to 2 days.

When you are ready to serve, preheat the oven to 180°C (350°F) Gas 4.

Dot the mozzarella over the top of the pasta mixture, then cover with foil and bake in the preheated oven for 30 minutes. After around 25 minutes, remove the foil to brown the top (alternatively, pop the pasta bake under a preheated hot grill/broiler for the last 5 minutes to brown the top).

Serve the pasta bake with the crispy salami alongside, on top or on the side.

4 slices salami

1 tablespoon olive oil

1 red onion, finely chopped

2 garlic cloves, finely chopped

1 courgette/zucchini, chopped

1 aubergine/eggplant, chopped

1 red (bell) pepper, deseeded and chopped

8–10 button/white mushrooms, chopped

2 tablespoons tomato purée/ paste

1 tablespoon pesto

2 x 400-g/7-oz. cans of chopped tomatoes

8 handfuls of dried pasta

250 ml/1 cup crème fraîche/ sour cream

200 g/7 oz. mozzarella cheese, torn into pieces

sea salt and freshly ground black pepper

SERVES 4

Risotto nero with garlic prawns/shrimp

A well-made risotto is always a treat. Black rice, cooked with squid ink and flavoured with fish stock, combined with pink prawns/shrimp makes a striking dish – one that tastes as good as it looks and is ideal for dinner parties.

1 litre/4 cups good-quality or homemade fish stock

3 tablespoons olive oil

1 shallot, finely chopped

3 garlic cloves, 2 finely chopped and 1 peeled but left whole

200-g/7-oz. squid, cleaned and chopped into small pieces

8-g/$^1/_4$-fl.oz. sachet of squid ink

350 g/1$^3/_4$ cups risotto rice, such as arborio

50 ml/3$^1/_2$ tablespoons dry white wine

25 g /1$^3/_4$ tablespoons butter

12 raw tiger prawns/shrimp, heads removed, peeled and deveined

sea salt

freshly chopped parsley, to garnish

SERVES 4

Bring the fish stock to a simmer in a large pan. Heat 2 tablespoons of the olive oil in a separate, heavy-based saucepan. Add the shallot and chopped garlic and fry gently, stirring, until the shallot has softened. Add the squid and fry, continuing to stir, until whitened and opaque. Mix in the squid ink. Stir in the rice. Pour over the wine and cook, stirring, until reduced.

Add a ladleful of the simmering stock to the rice and cook, stirring, until absorbed. Repeat the process until all the stock has been added and the rice is cooked through. Taste and season with salt as needed. Stir in the butter and set aside to rest briefly.

Heat the remaining oil in a frying pan/skillet. Once frothing, add the whole garlic clove and fry, stirring, until fragrant. Add the prawns/shrimp with a pinch of salt and fry, stirring, until the prawns/shrimp have turned pink and opaque and are cooked through. Discard the garlic clove. Serve the risotto rice topped with prawns/shrimp and parsley.

Spaghetti alle vongole

One for shellfish lovers, this simple yet classic pasta dish offers a taste of the sea, Italian style. Fresh clams have a distinctive sweetness and texture, flavoured here simply but effectively with olive oil, garlic, white wine and parsley.

1 kg/2 lbs. 3 oz. fresh clams

400 g/14 oz. spaghetti

6 tablespoons olive oil

3 garlic cloves, finely sliced lengthways

6 tablespoons finely chopped fresh parsley

100 ml/¹/₃ cup dry white wine

sea salt and freshly ground black pepper

SERVES 4

Prepare the clams by rinsing them under running water and sorting through, discarding any that are open. Keep in the fridge until you are ready to cook them.

Bring a large pan of salted water to the boil. Add the spaghetti and cook until al dente; drain.

Meanwhile, heat the olive oil in a large saucepan. Add the garlic and fry gently until just golden, stirring often. Take care not to burn the garlic, as this would give a bitter flavour. Add the clams, 2 tablespoons of the chopped parsley and the white wine.

Cover and cook for a few minutes until the clams have opened. Discard any that remain closed. Season with pepper.

Toss together the cooked spaghetti, clams and remaining parsley, adding just enough of the clam cooking liquor to moisten the spaghetti. Serve at once.

Goats' cheese and marjoram ravioli marinara

The marinara, or mariners' sauce, is simple and balances well with the salty goats' cheese and fragrant marjoram of the ravioli. Wonton wrappers make a brilliant cheat's ravioli pasta and can be found in the freezer in Asian supermarkets. You can prepare the ravioli up to three days ahead.

250 g/9 oz. soft goats' cheese

a large bunch of fresh marjoram

32 x 10-cm/4-in. square wonton wrappers

2 eggs, beaten

freshly grated Parmesan cheese, to serve

table salt, to season

MARINARA SAUCE

2 garlic cloves, crushed

50 ml/3½ tablespoons extra virgin olive oil

400 g/2 cups canned chopped tomatoes

200 ml/¾ cup vegetable stock

2 teaspoons capers

SERVES 4

Put the goats' cheese, two-thirds of the chopped marjoram leaves and a pinch of salt in a large mixing bowl and stir together.

Lay half of the wonton wrappers on a clean work surface and paint the edges with beaten egg. Spoon 1 tablespoon of the cheese mixture in the middle of each egg-washed wrapper, then lay the other half of the wonton wrappers on top. Gently press together to remove any air. Leave the ravioli to dry for 10 minutes or so. If you're making them in advance, put them in an airtight container, using baking parchment between each ravioli to stop them sticking.

To make the marinara sauce, put the garlic and olive oil in a saucepan over a medium heat. Cook until the garlic is just starting to brown, then add the chopped tomatoes, stock and capers, and bring to a low simmer.

Bring a large pan of salted water to a rolling boil, then gently add the ravioli. Maintain a low simmer for 3 minutes, then carefully remove the ravioli and place four on each serving plate. Spoon over the marinara sauce, decorate with a few marjoram leaves and sprinkle with Parmesan cheese.

Pesto alla genovese

Real Italian pesto is an exuberantly intense, rich paste of garlic, basil and cheese, given extra texture with pine nuts. Ligurians take pride in this culinary masterpiece: they say that the basil in their part of the Mediterranean has particular pungency. Pesto is best when it's made and eaten fresh.

125 g/1 cup pine nuts, lightly pan-toasted

6 garlic cloves, crushed then chopped

50 g/1$\frac{1}{2}$ cups fresh basil leaves, torn (2 large handfuls)

1 teaspoon sea salt

50 g/$\frac{2}{3}$ cup freshly grated Parmesan cheese

50 g/$\frac{2}{3}$ cup freshly grated pecorino cheese

150 ml/$\frac{2}{3}$ cup extra virgin olive oil

MAKES 250 ML/1 CUP

Grind the pine nuts, garlic, basil and salt to a paste with a mortar and pestle or in a food processor, using the pulse button.

Keep stirring the paste with one hand (or have the machine still running) while you gradually add half the cheese, then half the olive oil. Repeat the process until you have a rich, stiff, vividly green paste or sauce.

Use within hours if possible (though it keeps, sealed in an airtight container in the refrigerator, for up to 1 week).

Pasta with Pesto

Bring a large saucepan of water to the boil, then add a large pinch of salt. Add 8 small potatoes, halved, and cook for 5 minutes. Add 350 g/12 oz. dried trenette or tagliatelle and cook until al dente, about 8 minutes more. After about 4 minutes, add 1–2 handfuls of thin green beans. Drain, transfer to a large serving bowl, add about 125 ml/$\frac{1}{2}$ cup of the fresh pesto, toss well and serve.

Gnocchi with Pesto

Bring a large saucepan of water to the boil, then add a large pinch of salt. Add 500 g/1 lb. potato gnocchi and cook until they float to the surface and are chewy textured and well heated right through. Drain, transfer to a large serving bowl, add about 125 ml/$\frac{1}{2}$ cup of the fresh pesto, toss well and serve.

Alternatively, divide between 4 shallow earthenware dishes, set under a preheated grill/broiler and cook until bubbling, browned and aromatic.

Gnocchi with tomato, parsley and almonds

Gnocchi is a lovely alternative to pasta and is easy to make — you just have to make sure you only add just enough flour to bring the potato together, otherwise it can become overly chewy.

Preheat the oven to 200°C (400°F) Gas 6. Prick the potatoes and bake in the oven for about an hour or until fully cooked and tender. Remove from the oven (leave it on), and while still hot, using a knife, fork and spoon if necessary, cut open the potato and scoop the flesh into a bowl — you should have about 320 g/1²⁄₃ cups. Mash very well and then press through a sieve/strainer. Season with the nutmeg, ½ teaspoon finely ground sea salt and black pepper, then stir in most of the egg. Add in the flour a few spoonfuls at a time, and knead until you have a smooth dough. Depending on how wet the dough is, you may need a little more or less of the egg and flour, so add it in bit by bit to get it just right, smooth, but not sticky. Divide the dough into 4, and roll each piece into long sausage shapes, a little less then 2.5 cm/1 in. wide. Use some flour to prevent it from sticking. Cut into little lengths, about 2.5 cm/ 1 in. for each one. Using a floured fork, press down onto each piece to leave little ridges and shape into rectangles.

Place a large saucepan of water on to boil. While that is heating up, make the sauce by tossing the tomatoes with a little oil and place on a baking sheet in the oven for 12–15 minutes until their skins burst open. In the last 6 minutes, add the almonds to the oven on a separate baking sheet. Remove both from the oven and add to a food processor with the anchovies, garlic, capers, most of the parsley and 4½ tablespoons olive oil. Blitz until the almonds have broken into small pieces. Taste and adjust the seasoning if necessary.

Cook the gnocchi in batches in the boiling water. Stir in and boil for a couple of minutes or until they rise to the top. Strain thoroughly and gently combine together with the tomato sauce. Plate up with the remaining parsley sprinkled over and a little drizzle of extra virgin olive oil.

500 g/1 lb. evenly sized floury potatoes, like Désirée, Maris Piper or russets

½ teaspoon finely grated nutmeg

1 egg, beaten

125 g/1 cup white spelt flour

200 g/6½ oz. cherry tomatoes

extra virgin olive oil

40 g/¼ cup almonds

4 anchovy fillets

2 garlic cloves

2 teaspoons capers, rinsed thoroughly and drained

sea salt and freshly ground black pepper

a handful of fresh flat-leaf parsley leaves

SERVES 4

Lemon pepper ricotta gnocchi

A wonderful artisanal gnocchi that you will make over and over again. The flavours are gentle and fresh with a little kick from the pepper. Dusted in lashings of Parmesan and drizzled with good olive oil and fresh lemon, it is a perfect dish all year round, as a simple spring supper or a hearty dinner served alongside short ribs or stews.

450 g/2 cups ricotta cheese

grated zest of 2 large lemons

20 g/¼ cup freshly grated Parmesan cheese, plus extra to serve

100 g/¾ cup plain/all-purpose flour, plus extra for dusting

1 large egg, beaten

½ teaspoon ground white pepper, plus extra for dusting

½ teaspoon sea salt

extra virgin olive oil

20 g/½ cup torn mixed fresh herbs of your choice

SERVES 4–6

In a large bowl mix the ricotta, half the lemon zest, Parmesan, flour, egg, pepper and salt until well combined.

Turn out onto a work surface lightly dusted with flour and roll into a ball.

Divide into four pieces. Taking one piece at a time, roll into a thin sausage shape.

Repeat with the other pieces. Using a sharp knife, cut the dough into pieces 2.5 cm/1 in. long.

Bring a large pasta pot of salted water to the boil. Add the gnocchi and cook for a few minutes. They will float to the surface when cooked.

Drain and toss into a large bowl. Drizzle liberally with olive oil and add the remaining lemon zest, extra Parmesan and the herbs. Toss and serve in bowls with a dusting of white pepper to finish.

Spaghetti con aglio, olio e peperoncino

So simple but so good, this homely pasta dish of garlic, oil and chilli/chile is an Italian classic. Made in minutes using store-cupboard staples, it's a great speedy meal. A generous quantity of garlic is traditional as it is the dish's key flavouring.

Cook the spaghetti in a large pan of salted, boiling water until it becomes al dente.

Meanwhile, heat the olive oil in a small, heavy-based frying pan/skillet. Add the garlic and peperoncini and fry gently over a low heat, stirring often, until the garlic turns golden brown. Take care not to burn the garlic as this would make it bitter. Set the garlic pepperoncini oil aside to infuse.

Once the spaghetti is cooked, drain well and return to the saucepan. Gently reheat the oil and pour over the spaghetti, mixing well. Sprinkle with parsley and serve at once with Parmesan cheese.

450 g/1 lb. spaghetti

150 ml/²⁄₃ cup extra virgin olive oil

8 garlic cloves, finely chopped

6 peperoncini (small Italian dried chilli/chile peppers), chopped

6 tablespoons finely chopped fresh parsley

sea salt and freshly ground black pepper

grated Parmesan cheese, to serve

SERVES 4

Wild garlic/ramps pasta primavera

Primavera means 'spring' in Italian and this simple yet elegant recipe makes use of seasonal ingredients to create a lovely fresh and light garlicky pasta dish.

1 tablespoon pine nuts

100 g/1 cup fresh asparagus, sliced into 2.5-cm/1-in. lengths

75 g/1/2 cup fresh peas (or frozen if preferred)

75 g/2/3 cup green/French beans, topped, tailed and sliced into short lengths

200 g/3 cups farfalle pasta

100 g/1/2 cup Wild Garlic/Ramps Hazelnut Pesto

2 heaped tablespoons mascarpone cheese

grated Parmesan cheese, to serve

WILD GARLIC/RAMPS HAZELNUT PESTO

80 g/2/3 cup hazelnuts

80 g/3 oz. wild garlic leaves/ramps, thoroughly rinsed, roughly chopped

150 ml/2/3 cup extra virgin olive oil

50 g/2/3 cup grated Parmesan cheese

salt

SERVES 4

To make the pesto, dry-fry the hazelnuts in a heavy-based frying pan/skillet over a medium heat, stirring frequently, until golden brown. Set aside to cool, then finely grind.

If using a food processor, blitz the wild garlic/ramps into a paste. Add the ground hazelnuts and olive oil and briefly whizz together. Mix in the Parmesan cheese, then season with salt.

If using a pestle and mortar, pound the wild garlic/ramps into a paste. Add in the ground hazelnuts and olive oil and pound to mix together. Mix in the Parmesan cheese, then season with salt.

The left over pesto can be stored in the fridge for up to 2 days.

Put the pine nuts in a dry heavy-based frying pan/skillet set over a medium heat and toast, stirring often, until golden brown. Remove the pan from the heat and set aside.

Cook the asparagus, peas and green/French beans in separate pans of boiling water until just tender – you want them al dente. Drain at once, immerse in cold water to stop the cooking process, then drain again thoroughly.

Bring a large pan of salted water to the boil. Add the pasta and cook until al dente; drain.

Toss the freshly drained pasta first with the wild garlic/ramps pesto, then the mascarpone cheese, coating well. Add the asparagus, peas and green/French beans and toss together thoroughly. Scatter over the toasted pine nuts and serve at once, with Parmesan cheese sprinkled over the top.

Crab, tomato and basil linguine

Very quick to cook, this simple combination makes a stylish pasta dish.
Serve as a main course accompanied by a crisp-textured side salad.

Begin by scalding the tomatoes. Pour boiling water over the ripe tomatoes in a heatproof bowl. Set aside for 1 minute, then drain and carefully peel off the skin using a sharp knife. Halve the tomatoes, scoop out the soft pulp and finely dice the tomato.

Bring a large saucepan or pot of salted water to the boil over a high heat. Add the linguine and cook for 8–10 minutes, until al dente. Drain and keep warm.

Meanwhile, heat the oil in a frying pan/skillet set over a medium heat. Add the garlic and fry briefly until fragrant. Then add the crab meat, chilli/chile and wine. Season with pepper and cook, stirring, for 2–3 minutes until the wine has cooked down to form a sauce. Stir in the diced tomato.

Toss together the drained linguine, sauce and basil, ensuring the pasta is well coated in sauce. Serve at once.

250 g/½ lb. ripe tomatoes

400 g/14 oz. linguine

4 tablespoons olive oil

2 garlic cloves, peeled and finely chopped

300 g/10 oz. fresh crab meat (white and brown)

1 red chilli/chile, finely chopped

50 ml/1¾ oz. dry white wine

freshly ground black pepper

a handful of fresh basil leaves, shredded

SERVES 4

Pissaladière with provençal olive relish

The saltiness of the anchovies and sweetness of the caramelized onions
with olive relish is sensational. A taste of the south of France.

Begin by making the dough. Place the flour, yeast, thyme and salt in a ceramic bowl, and mix together. Stir in the water and 60 ml/¼ cup oil until combined. Cover with paper towels or clingfilm/plastic wrap and set aside to rise for 2½–3 hours until it doubles in size.

To make the Provençal Olive Relish place all the ingredients in a food processor and blend until the mixture is almost smooth but still has some texture. Season with pepper. Pack the relish into a sterilized glass jar and drizzle a little olive oil to cover the surface.

To caramelize the onions, place a large frying pan/skillet over medium–low heat and add the remaining olive oil and the onions. Cook for about 25 minutes,

stirring occasionally, until the onions are golden brown and soft. Set aside.

Preheat the oven to 500°F (260°C) Gas 10, or as high as it will go.

Oil a baking sheet and turn the risen dough onto it. Gently press the dough with palms of your hands, stretching it to the edges of the pan. Spread the onions over the dough and randomly dollop the Provençal Olive Relish on top. Arrange the anchovies and olives on top.

Bake in the preheated oven for about 15–20 minutes, until the dough is golden and crispy. Remove from the oven and slice into portions.

Serve garnished with sprigs of thyme and a drizzle of olive oil.

375 g/3 cups plain/all-purpose flour

7 g/¼ oz. active dry/fast action yeast

2 tablespoons fresh thyme leaves

½ teaspoon sea salt

300 ml/1¼ cups warm water

125 ml/½ cup olive oil, plus extra to serve

8 red onions, peeled and thinly sliced

12–14 anchovy fillets

15 pitted black olives

fresh thyme sprigs, to garnish

PROVENÇAL OLIVE RELISH

200 g/2 cups pitted Kalamata olives, drained

12 anchovy fillets

40 g/¼ cup capers, drained

grated zest and juice of 1 lemon

60 ml/¼ cup extra virgin olive oil, plus extra to cover

coarsely ground black pepper

sterilized glass jar with airtight lid (see page 4)

a baking sheet, greased

SERVES 6

Potato pizza

In general, Italians like to stick to the classics when it comes to pizza, but as you can see below, pizza toppings are limitless. This pizza has been inspired by a dish from Verona – well, it's just bread and cheese after all, isn't it?

15 g/ $^{1}/_{2}$ oz. fresh yeast, 1 tablespoon dried active baking yeast, or 1 sachet easy-blend yeast

a pinch of sugar

250 ml/1 cup warm water

350 g/2$^{1}/_{3}$ cups plain white flour, plus extra for dusting

1 tablespoon olive oil

a pinch of sea salt

POTATO TOPPING

1 medium potato, peeled and sliced extremely thinly

150 g/6 oz. Fontina, Taleggio or mozzarella cheese

1 large radicchio, cut into about 8 wedges, brushed with olive oil and grilled for 5 minutes

1 tablespoon chopped fresh thyme

sea salt and freshly ground black pepper

extra olive oil, for trickling

a baking pan, 23 x 33 cm/ 11 x 13 in., greased

SERVES 2–4, DEPENDING ON APPETITE

To make the dough, put the fresh yeast and sugar in a medium bowl and beat until creamy. Whisk in the warm water and leave for 10 minutes until frothy. For other yeasts, use according to the packet instructions.

Sift the flour into a large bowl and make a hollow in the centre. Pour in the yeast mixture, olive oil and a good pinch of salt. Mix with a round-bladed knife, then your hands, until the dough comes together. Transfer to a floured surface, wash and dry your hands and knead for 10 minutes until smooth and elastic. The dough should be quite soft, but if too soft to handle, add more flour, 1 tablespoon at a time. Put the dough in a clean, oiled bowl, cover with a damp kitchen towel or clingfilm/ plastic wrap and let rise until doubled in size – about 1 hour.

When risen, punch down the dough with your fists, then roll out or pat into a rectangle that will fit in the baking pan, pushing it up the sides a little. Cover the top with a thin layer of sliced potato, then half the cheese, the wedges of radicchio, then the remaining cheese. Season with salt and pepper, and sprinkle with thyme.

Preheat the oven to 220°C (425°F) Gas 7.

Trickle oil over the top and let rise in a warm place for 10 minutes. Bake in the preheated oven for 15–20 minutes or until golden and bubbling.

Caramelized red onion and salami pizza

What better way to celebrate salami than by putting it on an Italian pizza with Italian cheese? The look of the pepperoni pizza is often associated with cheap, poor-quality pizzas, but it is so different when you make it yourself and use good-quality ingredients. The ease of this recipe is that only the dough needs any preparation; the other ingredients are already prepared for you.

BASE/CRUST

170 g/1¹/₂ cups plain/
all-purpose or wholemeal/
whole-wheat flour

a small pinch of fast-action/
rapid-rise yeast

1 tablespoon olive oil

a pinch of sea salt

2 teaspoons caster/granulated
sugar

TOPPING

1 x 400-g/14-oz. can
tomatoes, drained and
chopped

1 tablespoon tomato purée/
paste

a big pinch of freshly chopped
parsley

a big pinch of freshly chopped
or dried oregano

about 40 g/1¹/₂ oz.
Caramelized Red Onions

150 g/5 oz. mozzarella
cheese, torn into pieces

8–10 slices salami or saucisson
sec

50 g/2 oz. pecorino cheese,
grated or shaved

a few fresh basil leaves

CARAMELIZED RED
ONIONS

1 red onion, thinly sliced

2 tablespoons runny honey

sea salt and freshly ground
black pepper

a large baking sheet, greased
or lined with parchment
paper

MAKES 1 PIZZA

Preheat the oven to 180°C (350°F) Gas 4.

Put the onion in an ovenproof dish, drizzle over the honey and stir to mix so that the onions are well coated. Roast in the preheated oven for 15 minutes, until caramelized. Set aside.

For the base/crust, put all the ingredients in a bowl, add 125 ml/ ¹/₂ cup water and mix together with your hands to make a dough. If the mixture feels sloppy, just add a little more flour, or add a little more water for the opposite (it shouldn't be so dry that it crumbles when you roll it). Turn the dough out onto a flour-dusted surface and knead for 5–10 minutes, until smooth and elastic. The kneading is always a bit boring but just remember that you need (groan!) to do it or your base will be chewy and tough. If you have a bread maker, it will do the work for you – just follow the timing instructions for your machine.

Place the dough back in the bowl and cover with a damp kitchen towel for about 1 hour, until risen slightly.

Transfer the dough to a flour-dusted surface and punch it down gently to release the air. Roll out the dough to a large round. Put the pizza base/crust on the prepared baking sheet and bake in the preheated oven for 10 minutes, turning over halfway through. It really helps to part-bake the base/crust

on its own like this first, so that you don't have to bake it for too long with the topping on (and risk the topping burning).

Meanwhile, prepare the topping. Mix the canned tomatoes, tomato purée/paste, parsley and oregano in a bowl, and season with salt and pepper.

Remove the pizza base/crust from the oven and turn it over so the softer side that was touching the baking sheet is now facing up. Spread the tomato mixture evenly over the top and then spoon over the caramelized onions, if using. Distribute the mozzarella cheese over the tomato mixture, followed by the salami slices, and finally sprinkle over the pecorino cheese. Sprinkle the basil leaves on top.

Return the pizza to the preheated oven on the middle shelf (ideally, put the pizza directly onto the oven shelf, rather than using the baking sheet, so the base/crust can continue to crisp) and bake for a further 15 minutes, until the cheese has melted. Serve hot.

Tuna and anchovy pizza

The satisfaction of making your own pizza bases can't be underestimated and it is probably easier than you think. You can even make a batch of the pizzas, wrap and freeze them.

To make the pizza dough, combine the warm water, yeast, flour, salt and oil in a large mixing bowl. Bring the ingredients together into one ball using the tips of your fingers. Turn out onto an oiled worktop and with the base of your hand stretch and knead the dough for 10 minutes.

When the dough is a smooth and consistent texture, it's ready to prove. Drizzle a little oil into the base of a large bowl, oil the ball of dough and put in the bowl. Cover with a clean kitchen cloth and put the bowl somewhere warm (an airing cupboard is ideal for this) for 1½ hours.

Preheat the oven to 220°C (425°F) Gas 7.

Once proved, the dough should be at least twice its original size. Gently turn it out onto an oiled surface and knead the dough gently to knock out the air. Divide it into four portions. Put each of the pieces of dough onto a separate prepared baking sheet and stretch the dough with your fingertips until it is about 5 mm/¼ in. thick. Don't worry about making the base completely even as thinner or thicker areas add to the flavour and texture of the finished pizza.

Bake each base (one at a time depending on the size of your oven) in the preheated oven for 6 minutes. Remove them from the baking sheets

and put back in the oven, directly on the oven shelf, to cook for another 3 minutes.

To finish, spread 15 g/1 tablespoon of tomato purée/paste on each pizza base and sprinkle evenly with the cheeses. Place the anchovies evenly across each pizza and do the same with the tuna and the red onion. Return the pizzas to the oven, directly on the oven shelf, for 10 minutes.

Sprinkle with freshly chopped tarragon, slice and serve immediately.

Tip

To freeze the pizzas cook for only 6 minutes of the final cooking time, then remove from the oven and set aside to cool completely. Place in a large sealable bag and freeze. To cook from frozen, preheat the oven to 220°C (425°F) Gas 7 and cook, directly on the oven shelf, for 6 minutes.

180 ml/¾ cup warm water

5 g/¼ oz. fast-action dried/active dry yeast

300 g/2⅓ cups strong bread flour

1 teaspoon sea salt

40 ml/3 tablespoons extra virgin olive oil, plus extra to drizzle

TOPPINGS

60 g/4 tablespoons tomato purée/paste

200 g/1½ cups grated mozzarella cheese

200 g/2 cups grated Cheddar cheese

50 g/½ cup grated Parmesan cheese

50 g/½ cup canned anchovies in oil

160 g/⅔ cup canned tuna in spring water

1 red onion, finely chopped

a small bunch of fresh tarragon

4 baking sheets, oiled

SERVES 4

Falsomagro beef and pork

Falsomagro translates as 'fake lean'. It's unclear why this dish has the name – perhaps it's because there is a lot of stuffing and only a little meat in the portions served.

Boil the eggs for 6 minutes, then shell them, slice them and set aside.

Prepare the stuffing for the roast by mixing the minced/ground pork with the skinned sausages. Sauté for 10 minutes in a small quantity of oil, adding half the onion.

Lay out the slices of beef on the work surface, in a rectangle and overlapping them slightly. Spread with the sautéed pork and sausage meat mixture. Add the slices of bacon, the sliced hard-boiled/hard-cooked eggs, pecorino cheese and garlic, then season with salt and pepper. Roll up into a long sausage shape and tie with kitchen string/twine in several places along the length, to prevent it unwrapping.

Put some oil and the rest of the sliced onion in a casserole dish over medium heat. Add the stuffed roast and brown all over. Pour over the red wine and let it evaporate, then lower the heat and continue to cook uncovered for 1 hour, adding stock a little at a time.

Serve in thick slices, with the onions and sauce.

2 eggs

150 g/5¹/₂ oz. lean minced/ground pork

2 Sicilian-style sausages or other good-quality pork sausages (remove casing)

extra virgin olive oil

1 onion, sliced

800 g/1 lb. 12 oz. very thinly sliced sirloin beef

3 slices bacon

50 g/³/₄ cup freshly grated pecorino cheese

1 garlic clove, finely chopped

125 ml/¹/₂ cup red wine

vegetable or chicken stock, as required approx. 500 ml/2 cups in total

sea salt and freshly ground black pepper

SERVES 4–6

Spanish duck with olives

Duck with olives has always been a famous Spanish, French and Italian delicacy, and both main ingredients are often of high quality in all three countries. Instead of using a whole duck, cut into pieces, this recipe uses 'magrets' or boneless breast portions. The skin is left on but is slashed to brown well.

2 large magrets (boneless breast portions) of muscovy or other duck about 500 g/1 lb.

1 teaspoon roughly crushed black pepper

1/2 teaspoon sea salt

4 garlic cloves, finely chopped then crushed

8 shallots or pearl onions

6 tablespoons Pedro Ximenez sherry (or other aged sweet sherry) or 4 tablespoons pomegranate molasses

40 whole, or pitted and stuffed green olives (with anchovies, lemon zest or almonds)

4 tablespoons chicken or beef consommé, or rich stock

750 g/1 1/2 cups cooked (or canned) white beans, lentils or chickpeas/garbanzo beans, drained

2 tablespoons fresh herbs, such as parsley and celery tops

SERVES 4

Preheat a ridged stovetop grill pan until very hot. Pat the duck breasts dry with paper towels.

Mix the pepper and salt and half of the garlic to a paste. Rub some all over the duck breasts. Make 3 diagonal slashes on the skin side of each breast, then cook, skin side down, for 2 minutes. Reduce the heat to moderate and continue to cook until the fat runs and the surface is darkly browned.

Pour out and reserve the fat, returning 1 tablespoon to the pan. Using tongs, turn the duck breasts over. Add the shallots and sherry. Cover and cook over low heat for a further 4–6 minutes or until the duck is rare or medium-rare, depending on your taste.

Add the olives and another tablespoon of duck fat to the sauce. Remove the duck breasts and keep them warm. Add the consommé to the pan. Shake and stir the pan contents until the sauce becomes a rich syrupy glaze.

Put the beans in a saucepan and crush coarsely with a fork or potato masher. Stir in 2 tablespoons of the duck fat, salt, pepper, herbs and the remaining garlic and heat through.

Cut the duck widthways or diagonally into thin slices. Serve with a trickle of sauce and a mound of the mashed beans.

Sicilian tuna

This famous Sicilian fish dish is best made with a tail piece of fresh tuna, but you can use any large dense portion of the right weight. It must be skinless, boneless and perfectly trimmed. Tuna cooks to a dense texture: although this dish is not rare-cooked, do try to cook it just until set, so that it is still moist and delicious. Serve with crispy flatbreads or sliced country bread. A lively, fruity, dry white wine would suit.

1.75 kg/3¹/₂–4 lbs. boneless, skinless, trimmed tail section of fresh tuna

8 garlic cloves, 4 chopped then mashed, 4 left whole

1 unwaxed lemon, zest removed in 1-cm/ ¹/₂-in. strips

24 sprigs of mint or leaves, plus extra to serve

25 g/2 tablespoons unsalted butter

4 tablespoons extra virgin olive oil

about 900 g/28 oz. canned tomatoes in tomato juice

60 ml/¹/₄ cup fish stock

60 ml/¹/₄ cup white wine

16 small pearl onions

sea salt and freshly ground black pepper

SERVES 6–8

Pat the tuna dry with paper towels. Slice the 4 whole garlic cloves into 6 long strips each, making 24. Cut the lemon zest into 24 pieces. Starting from the centre top, cut a series of 8 incisions in the fish, using a small, sharp knife and keep the point in position while you push a strip of garlic, a mint sprig and a bit of zest into each incision.

Repeat the process twice more along each side, making 2 further rows of incisions and filling them as described. Using your fingers or a pastry brush, rub the mashed garlic over the surface of the fish.

Heat the butter and oil in a large flameproof casserole and brown the tuna all over for 10 minutes, using tongs to position it. Add the tomatoes, their juice and fish stock and bring to the boil. Cover the pan, reduce the heat and simmer for 10 minutes. Add the white wine and pearl onions and cook for

15 minutes longer. Remove the fish, keep it warm and leave it to 'rest'.

Bring the tomato liquid to the boil over high heat, and cook, stirring often, until it has reduced to a thick, rich red sauce. Add salt and pepper to taste. If you like, put it in a blender and purée until smooth.

Return the fish to its sauce in the casserole for about 10 minutes or until heated through. Remove it and carve into 1 cm/¹/₂ in. slices. Serve on a bed of tomato sauce with extra mint leaves.

Note

Serve the extra sauce with rice, noodles or gnocchi, as a separate course, before or after this course, or the next day.

Lamb steaks with cherry tomato and anchovy sauce

This tangy sauce, flavoured with savoury anchovies and garlic, is an excellent partner for griddled lamb. Serve with new potatoes and green beans for a simple but satisfying meal.

250 g/¹/₂ lb. cherry tomatoes

1 tablespoon olive oil, plus extra for brushing

1 large garlic clove, sliced

4 anchovy fillets in oil, chopped

4 lamb steaks

sea salt and freshly ground black pepper

SERVES 4

Begin by scalding the tomatoes. Pour boiling water over the ripe tomatoes in a heatproof bowl. Set aside for 1 minute, then drain and carefully peel off the skin using a sharp knife. Slice in half and set aside.

Heat the oil in a small, heavy-bottomed frying pan/skillet set over a low heat.

Add the garlic and fry, stirring often, for 1 minute until fragrant. Add the anchovy fillets and continue to fry, stirring continuously, until they melt into the oil. Add the tomato halves and cook, stirring now and then, until the tomatoes have softened to form a sauce. Season with pepper and keep warm until ready to serve.

Preheat a ridged stovetop grill pan over a medium heat.

Season the lamb steaks with salt and pepper, and brush with oil.

Cook the lamb steaks in the hot pan as desired.

Serve the grilled steaks with the warm cherry tomato anchovy sauce.

Sweet treats and drinks

From the refreshing blood orange granita from Sicily to an elegant French lemon tart and Italy's finest gelato plus the wickedly refreshing limoncello, the Mediterranean offers the most delicious ways with which to round off any meal.

Chocolate cherry amaretti

These wonderful little treats are very noticeable in pasticceria (confectioners' shops), particularly in Syracusa, Sicily. They're best made 'a casa lingor' (at home).

Preheat the oven to 160°C (325°F) Gas 3.

Mix the almonds, caster/granulated sugar, chocolate, cherries and lemon zest together. Whisk the egg whites until firm and add to the almond mixture with the salt. Mix well. The mixture should be damp.

Sift the icing/confectioners' sugar into a bowl. Form balls with the almond mixture, about the size of three-quarters of a tablespoon. Roll in icing/confectioners' sugar and place on a parchment-lined baking sheet.

Bake in the preheated oven until they have a golden tinge, approximately 12–14 minutes. Cool on a wire rack.

250 g/2¹/₂ cups freshly ground almonds (for maximum flavour)

120 g/1¹/₄ cups caster/granulated sugar

50 g/¹/₂ cup dark/bittersweet chocolate, grated

60 g/¹/₂ cup dried cherries, chopped

finely grated zest of 1 lemon

2 UK large/US extra large egg whites

a pinch of sea salt

30 g/3¹/₂ tablespoons icing/confectioners' sugar

MAKES 12–14

Fluffy ricotta fritters

Deep-fried snacks like these are part of Italian life and are seen as a real festive treat. Fluffy little puffs like this are very popular, and are found in many guises. There is usually one to suit each saint for each Saint's Day.

Press the ricotta through a food mill, potato ricer or sieve/strainer into a large bowl. Put the eggs, sugar and vanilla in a second bowl and whisk until pale and light. Fold into the ricotta.

Sift the flour with the baking powder and salt into a bowl, then fold it into the cheese and egg mixture.

Heat the vegetable oil in the deep-fryer to 190°C (375°F). Have a tray lined with paper towels and a slotted spoon or strainer at the ready.

Drop level tablespoons of the mixture into the hot oil in batches of 6. Fry for 2–3 minutes until puffed and deep brown all over (you may have to turn them in the oil). Drain and serve immediately, dusted with icing/confectioners' sugar.

250 g/1 cup ricotta cheese

2 eggs, at room temperature

2 tablespoons sugar

1 teaspoon real vanilla essence

120 g/³/₄ cup plain/all-purpose flour

1 teaspoon baking powder

¹/₂ teaspoon sea salt

vegetable oil, for deep-frying

icing/confectioners' sugar, to serve

an electric deep-fryer

a tray lined with paper towels

SERVES 4–6

Amaretti with pine nuts

Delicious, crisp little cookies made with a mixture of freshly ground almonds and pine nuts. If you have any peach or apricot kernels, use these in place of some of the almonds and they will impart a fantastic almond flavour – in this case, don't add the almond essence. These are wonderful used as the base for a trifle or eaten with after-dinner liqueurs.

100 g/³/₄ cup blanched almonds

100 g/1 cup pine nuts, plus 3 tablespoons extra, to sprinkle

90 g/¹/₂ cup caster/granulated sugar

2 large egg whites

1 teaspoon almond essence

a piping bag fitted with a plain 1.25-cm/¹/₂-in. nozzle/tip

2 baking sheets lined with parchment paper

MAKES ABOUT 30

Put the almonds, pine nuts and 1 tablespoon of the caster/granulated sugar in a food processor fitted with the grater disc. Grind to a fine powder. Alternatively, use a blender or rotary nut grinder. Set aside.

Put the egg whites in a bowl and beat with a hand-held electric mixer until stiff but not dry. Gradually whisk in the remaining sugar until the whites are stiff and shiny. Fold in the ground nuts and almond essence. Spoon the mixture into the piping bag and pipe the mixture onto the baking sheets in tiny rounds.

Preheat the oven to 150°C (300°F) Gas 2.

Sprinkle with a few extra pine nuts and bake in the preheated oven for 30 minutes, until the biscuits are lightly browned and hard. Transfer to a wire rack to cool. Store in an airtight container for up to 2 weeks.

75 g/6 tablespoons icing/confectioners' sugar, sifted

175 g/1¹/₂ sticks butter, at room temperature

2 egg yolks

2 tablespoons iced water

250 g/1²/₃ cups plain/all-purpose flour, sifted

LEMON FILLING

4 eggs

150 g/³/₄ cup caster/superfine sugar

2 tablespoons grated lemon zest and 125 ml/¹/₂ cup freshly squeezed lemon juice from 2–3 lemons

100 ml/¹/₂ cup double/heavy cream, plus extra to serve

a shallow, loose bottom 20-cm/8-in. tart pan, no more than 3 cm/1 in. deep, set on a baking sheet

parchment paper and baking beans

SERVES 4

French lemon tart

Lemon tart – wobbly, sharp, creamy but acidic – is an outrageously delicious dish. In France, these are often slim, very elegant offerings, not heavily filled. The ideal is to make it a few hours before you intend to eat it.

To make the pastry, set aside 2 tablespoons of the icing/confectioners' sugar and put the remainder in the bowl of an electric mixer. Add the butter and beat until creamy, soft and white. Add the egg yolks one at a time and continue beating until well mixed. Trickle in half the iced water, then add the flour. Whisk on a lower speed, adding the remaining water until the pastry gathers into a soft ball. Wrap in clingfilm/plastic wrap, and chill for 40–60 minutes.

Transfer the pastry to a floured work surface and roll out to 5 mm/¹/₄ in. thick. Use it to line the tart pan. Gently push the dough into the corners. Cut off the excess pastry. Chill for a further 20 minutes or until very firm.

Preheat the oven to 180°C (350°F) Gas 4.

Prick the pastry all over with a fork, line with greaseproof paper, fill with baking beans and bake blind in the preheated oven for 15 minutes. Remove the paper and the beans. Let the pastry rest for 5 minutes, then bake again for 10 minutes or until pale golden. Cut off any excess pastry to make a neat edge.

To make the filling, put the eggs, sugar and half the lemon zest in a bowl and beat well for 2 minutes with an electric whisk. Stir in the lemon juice and cream, then pour the mixture into the tart shell. Bake at 120°C (250°F) Gas ¹/₂ for 35 minutes, or until the filling is barely set.

While the tart cooks, put the remaining lemon zest in a sieve/strainer, pour over boiling water, then refresh under cold running water. Put the zest, the reserved 2 tablespoons icing/confectioners' sugar and 4 tablespoons water in a saucepan over low heat. Cook gently until the zest looks syrupy. Sprinkle the zest over the cooked tart. Serve hot or warm, with additional spoonfuls of cream.

Strawberries with balsamic syrup and mascarpone ice cream

Strawberries with balsamic may sound strange, but this resinous syrup brings out their sweetness. Even the least flavoursome fruits taste better with a touch of balsamic.

To make the ice cream, put the milk in a saucepan. Split the vanilla pod/bean lengthways, scrape out the seeds and add the pod/bean and seeds to the milk. Heat until almost boiling, remove from the heat, stir well and set aside to infuse for 30 minutes.

Put the egg yolks and sugar in a bowl and whisk until pale and creamy. Add the milk and vanilla pod/bean and mix well. Return the mixture to the pan and remove the vanilla pod/bean (which can be rinsed, dried and used to flavour a jar of sugar). Cook the mixture over low heat, stirring constantly, until it is thick enough to coat the back of a wooden spoon. It must not boil or it will curdle. Remove from the heat and stir in the cream. Leave to cool completely.

When cold, use a hand-held electric mixer to beat the custard into the mascarpone. Chill, then freeze in an ice cream maker, transfer to a freezer container and store in the freezer.

To make the balsamic syrup, put the sugar, balsamic vinegar and 200 ml/ 1 cup water in a small saucepan. Heat gently until the sugar dissolves. Bring to the boil and boil rapidly for 5 minutes until reduced by one-quarter. Remove from the heat, cool, then chill.

Toss the strawberries in the syrup. Transfer the ice cream to the refrigerator at least 20 minutes before serving, to soften. Serve the strawberries with scoops of mascarpone ice cream, then trail any remaining syrup over the top.

650 g/1¹/₂ lbs. ripe strawberries, halved

MASCARPONE ICE CREAM

450 ml/2¹/₄ cups whole milk

1 vanilla pod/bean

5 large egg yolks

125 g/¹/₂ cup plus 2 tablespoons caster/ granulated sugar

300 ml/1¹/₂ cups double/heavy cream

300 g/1¹/₄ cups mascarpone cheese

BALSAMIC SYRUP

200 g/1 cup caster/superfine sugar

2 tablespoons balsamic vinegar

an ice cream maker

SERVES 4

Warm zabaglione with pears poached in Marsala

There is nothing quite as sensual as warm zabaglione served straight from the pan. The secret is not to let the mixture get too hot, though still hot enough to cook and thicken the egg yolks.

300 ml/1⅓ cups sweet white wine

300 ml/1⅓ cups Marsala wine

200 g/1 cup caster/granulated sugar

1 vanilla pod/bean, split, seeds scraped out and reserved

6 firm but ripe pears

1 teaspoon real vanilla essence

ZABAGLIONE

6 large egg yolks

6 tablespoons Marsala wine

6 tablespoons caster/granulated sugar to serve (optional)

chopped pan-toasted hazelnuts, to serve (optional)

mint leaves, to serve (optional)

SERVES 6

To poach the pears, put the white wine, Marsala, sugar and the split vanilla pod/bean and seeds into a saucepan and bring to the boil. Peel the fruit carefully, but leave their stalks on, and shave a thin slice from the base so the pears will stand up. Stand them in the wine in the saucepan – they should just fit. Spoon over a little liquid to prevent discoloration. Cover tightly and simmer for about 25 minutes, turning occasionally, until tender. Leave to cool in the liquid.

Remove the vanilla pod/bean. Lift out the pears and set in a serving dish. Boil the liquid until reduced to 300 ml/ 1¼ cups. Stir in the vanilla essence. Cool, then pour over the pears. Chill until ready to serve.

Make the zabaglione at the last minute. Put the egg yolks, Marsala and sugar in a medium heatproof bowl and beat with a hand-held electric mixer or a whisk until well blended. Set over a saucepan of gently simmering water – the base should at no time be in contact with the water. Do not let the water boil. Whisk the mixture until it is glossy, pale, light, fluffy and holds a trail when dropped from the whisk. This should take about 5 minutes. To serve, spoon a pool of syrup onto a plate, add 1–2 spoonfuls of zabaglione, then stand a pear on top.

Weekend chocolate cake with Armagnac prunes

This is a fun cake to make. Rich and decadent, and steeped in heavenly Armagnac syrup and prunes, it takes time to eat and savour – perfect for long, lazy lunches.

To make the Armagnac prunes, begin by preparing the prunes. In a non-reactive pan, bring the sugar and 475 ml/2 cups water to the boil over medium–high heat. Reduce the heat and simmer for 5 minutes, until the sugar has dissolved. Pour the syrup over the prunes in a large bowl, cover and soak for 12–14 hours, or overnight.

Once soaked, remove the cover and stir the Armagnac into the prunes in syrup. Pack the prunes into sterilized glass jars, leaving a 5-mm/¼-in. space at the top. Carefully tap the jars on the worktop to get rid of air pockets. Wipe the jars clean and tightly screw on the lids.

Preheat the oven to 180°C (350°F) Gas 4.

Sift the cocoa and flour together into a large bowl, and set aside.

Place the eggs and sugar in a electric stand mixer and beat on high for 5–6 minutes until light and fluffy. Reduce the speed of the mixer to slow, and add the cocoa and flour a little at a time. Add the pure vanilla extract, butter and chopped prunes, and mix until combined.

Pour the cake batter into the prepared cake pan and bake in the preheated oven for 35 minutes. Check it is cooked through by inserting a wooden to skewer into the middle of the cake: if it comes out clean, it's ready. Remove the cake from the oven and leave to cool in the pan on a wire rack. Prick the top of the cake all over with a wooden skewer.

To make the syrup, bring the sugar, 60 ml/¼ cup water, Armagnac and honey to the boil in a small saucepan over medium–high heat. Cook for 4–5 minutes, stirring occasionally, until it thickens. Pour the hot syrup over the cake, cover and set aside at room temperature for 12–14 hours or overnight.

The next day, remove the cake from the pan and place on a serving plate. Top with the whole prunes, and serve with a big bowl of mascarpone or crème fraîche.

85 g/⅔ cup good-quality cocoa powder

125 g/1 cup plain/all-purpose flour

8 eggs

250 g/1¼ cups light brown sugar

1 teaspoon pure vanilla extract

115 g/1 stick unsalted butter, melted

120 g/½ cup Armagnac Prunes finely chopped

mascarpone cheese, to serve

ARMAGNAC PRUNES

450 g/3½ cups dried prunes

2 tablespoons brown sugar

235 ml/1 cup Armagnac

sterilized glass jars with airtight lids (see page 4)

SYRUP

55 g/¼ cup brown sugar

60 ml/¼ cup Armagnac

85 g/¼ cup honey

225 g/1 cup Armagnac Prunes

a 25-cm/10-in. springform cake pan, buttered and floured

an electric stand mixer fitted with a paddle attachment

a wooden skewer cocktail stick or toothpick

SERVES 6–8

Orange syrup semolina cake
with crème fraîche

This soft, moist, buttery cake contrasts nicely with the tangy crème fraîche on the side and makes an excellent dessert, with a small espresso coffee on the side.

Preheat the oven to 180°C (350°F) Gas 4.

In a mixing bowl, cream together the butter and sugar until well-mixed. Add the orange zest and juice, then the eggs, one at a time, followed by the crème fraîche/sour cream and mix well. Add the flour, baking power, semolina and salt and fold in. Transfer to the cake pan and bake in the preheated oven for 1 hour until golden-brown.

While the cake is baking, prepare the orange syrup. Place the orange juice and sugar in a small saucepan and gently heat, stirring, until the sugar has dissolved. Turn off the heat and wait until the pan has cooled, then mix in the orange flower water.

Test whether or not the cake is ready by piercing with a fine skewer; if it comes out clean, the cake is cooked, if not, bake it for a few minutes longer.

Remove the cake from the oven and place it on a rimmed baking sheet. While warm, pierce the top of the cake all over with a skewer. Pour over the orange syrup, then cover the cake and set it aside to cool and soak up the syrup, a few hours or overnight. Serve with crème fraîche/sour cream.

150 g/10 tablespoons butter, softened

175 g/³/4 cup plus 2 tablespoons caster/ granulated sugar

grated zest and freshly squeezed juice of ¹/2 orange

2 eggs

100 ml/6 tablespoons crème fraîche/ sour cream

125 g/1 cup plain/all-purpose flour, sifted

1 teaspoon baking powder

125 g/1 cup plus 2 tablespoons fine semolina

a pinch of sea salt

ORANGE SYRUP

juice of 1 large orange

150 g/³/4 cup caster/granulated sugar

1 teaspoon orange flower water

crème fraîch/sour cream, to serve

a loose-based 20 cm/8 in. cake pan

SERVES 8

Panna cotta with rose petal syrup

In English, panna cotta simply means 'cooked cream', and essentially that is what it is, with some additional flavourings and setting agents. With hints of vanilla, almond and rose, this is a luxurious version. Scented syrup and rose petals are the final touch for a captivating taste of the sunny Mediterranean.

Put the gelatine in a heatproof bowl, add 4 tablespoons water and leave to swell.

Put the cream, vanilla pod/bean and its seeds in a small saucepan, heat to simmering, then almost to boiling, then turn off the heat. Leave to stand for 2 minutes.

Stir in the soaked gelatine until it dissolves. Remove the vanilla pod/bean.

Put the sugar, mascarpone, almond extract and $1/2$ teaspoon of the rosewater in a bowl and whisk until creamy and smooth. Whisk in the gelatine mixture. Pour into the prepared pots, cups or dishes and chill for at least 2 hours.

Meanwhile, to make the syrup, put the vanilla sugar and white wine in a small saucepan over gentle heat and stir until dissolved and bubbling. Leave to cool slightly, then stir in the remaining rosewater. Serve the panna cotta in their pots, or turned out, with a trickle of syrup and several scented rose petals, and crisp biscuits/cookies such as cantucci or amaretti.

1 sachet gelatine granules, about 7 g/1 tablespoon

150 ml/$^2/_3$ cup single/light cream

1 vanilla pod/bean, split lengthways, seeds removed with the point of a knife

75 g/$^1/_3$ cup caster/granulated sugar

500 g/1 lb. mascarpone cheese

$1/2$ teaspoon almond extract or 1 tablespoon Amaretto liqueur

1 teaspoon rosewater

SYRUP

25 g/2 tablespoons vanilla sugar

6–8 tablespoons white wine

TO SERVE

1 scented rose, pulled into petals

6–8 cantucci or amaretti biscuits/cookies (optional)

6–8 small pots, cups or dishes, oiled

SERVES 6–8

Fig and honey ricotta cheesecake

Ricotta makes for a pleasantly light-textured cheesecake. Here it's combined with figs and honey to give a Mediterranean flavour. Serve it for dessert or enjoy it with coffee as a mid-morning treat.

Preheat the oven to 180°C (350°F) Gas 4.

Using a rolling pin, crush the biscuits/crackers into crumbs.

Use a large bowl to mix the crumbs with the melted butter. Next, press this mixture firmly and evenly into the cake pan to form a base.

In a separate large bowl, mix together the ricotta and eggs. Stir in the honey, orange flower water and flour.

Spoon the ricotta mixture evenly across the biscuit base. Now, press the halved figs, skin-side down, into the ricotta mixture.

Bake the cheesecake in the preheated oven for 50 minutes to 1 hour until set. Remove the pan from the oven and cool, then cover and chill until serving.

The cheesecake will keep for a few days, covered, in the refrigerator.

150 g/5 oz. digestive biscuits/graham crackers

50 g/$3^1/_2$ tablespoons butter, melted

750 g/3 cups ricotta cheese

2 eggs

2 tablespoons runny honey

$^1/_2$ teaspoon orange flower water

40 g/$^1/_3$ cup plain/all-purpose flour

6 fresh figs, halved

20-cm/8-in. loose-based cake pan

SERVES 6

Honey parfait with meringue and caramelized pistachios

You don't need any special equipment to make a really fantastic frozen dessert, as this recipe will prove. It is also easy, fast and probably takes first place ahead of all the other recipes in this book. Hard to believe, but this is better than chocolate cake. You can also freeze it in individual silicone moulds.

100 g/1 cup shelled pistachio nuts

50 g/¼ cup sugar

300 ml/1¼ cups whipping/heavy cream, chilled

2 large eggs, separated

100 g/scant ⅓ cup clear honey

8–10 mini meringues or 6–8 meringue nests

a loaf pan or other freezerproof mould

SERVES 6

Put the pistachios and sugar in a non-stick saucepan. Cook over medium–high heat, stirring, until they begin to caramelize. Remove from the pan and leave to cool. Grind coarsely in a food processor or by putting between 2 sheets of baking parchment and crushing with a rolling pin.

Put the cream in a large bowl and whisk until firm. Set aside. Put the egg yolks and honey in a second bowl, whisk well, then set aside. Put the egg whites in a third bowl and beat until they hold stiff peaks. Set aside.

Fold the egg yolk mixture into the cream until blended. Gently fold in the egg whites until just blended. Fold in the pistachios.

Spoon half the mixture into a freezerproof mould. Arrange the meringues on top in a single layer – nests may have to be broken up slightly depending on size, but not too small, because you want big pieces of meringue in the finished dish. Cover with the remaining parfait mixture and smooth the top. Cover with clingfilm/plastic wrap and freeze for about 6–8 hours or overnight, until firm. Scoop into tall glasses to serve.

Spanish flans

These superb caramelized egg custards scented with strips of lemon zest, are one of the joys of Spain. This version is from Catalonia. Often they are made in small, shallow, individual earthenware dishes, glazed on the inside. Catalonia once briefly included Sicily, Sardinia and Naples, so there are interesting culinary influences from these neighbouring cuisines. This version is lighter than the French variety, crème caramel, and tastes wonderful.

150 ml/²/₃ cup single/light cream and milk, mixed half and half

zest of 1 lemon, cut into 8 long strips, bruised

50 g/¹/₄ cup caster/granulated sugar

3 eggs

2 teaspoons vanilla extract

4 tablespoons caster/granulated sugar, to glaze

4 shallow heatproof dishes, 80 ml/¹/₃ cup each

a baking pan

a cook's blowtorch (optional)

SERVES 4

Put the cream, milk and 4 of the strips of lemon zest in a saucepan and heat almost to boiling (this is called scalding). Put the pan in a bowl of iced water to cool it quickly. Put the sugar, eggs and vanilla in a bowl and whisk until well blended, trying to avoid making froth. Stir in the cooled scalded cream.

Pour the custard mixture into the 4 dishes. Add the remaining strips of lemon zest: tuck one into each custard.

Preheat the oven to 150°C (300°F) Gas 2

Set the dishes in a baking pan and add enough boiling water to come halfway up the sides of the dishes. Bake towards the top of the preheated oven for 20 minutes or until very gently set and wobbly. Remove the baking pan from the oven, then remove the dishes from the pan.

Sprinkle the sugar evenly over each custard. Preheat an overhead grill/broiler to very hot, leaving space for the pots to be 3 cm/1 in. from the heat. Alternatively turn on the blowtorch. Grill or blowtorch the custards until a fine layer of caramel forms on top. Serve, preferably at room temperature, within 2 hours.

Baklava

This recipe has been created in order to make something just as delicious as traditional baklava, but without all the refined cane sugar and butter. It uses coconut oil and maple syrup, which are just wonderful with the spices and nuts.

For the syrup, place all the ingredients in a saucepan and bring to the boil. Reduce the heat to low and simmer for 5 minutes until slightly reduced. Remove from the heat and leave to cool. Strain through a sieve/strainer and refrigerate.

Preheat the oven to 180°C (350°F) Gas 4. Place half the nuts and the coconut palm sugar, salt, ground cinnamon and cardamom in a food processor. Blitz until very finely chopped. Add in the remaining nuts and blitz until finely chopped, but not quite as finely as the first half, so they have a bit of a bite.

Using a pastry brush, brush the parchment paper with a little of the melted coconut butter or oil. Place one filo/phyllo sheet into the tray and generously brush with oil, but do not let it pool, repeat 5 times so you have 6 oiled sheets. Place half the nut mixture on top and gently spread out. Layer another 6 filo/phyllo sheets on top, oiling each sheet generously. Spread the rest of the nut mixture on top and finish with the last 8 sheets of filo/phyllo, brushing with oil as before. Press firmly down on the baklava so it is well compacted.

Using a very sharp knife, cut the baklava into bite-sized rectangle or diamond shapes, take your time so as not to tear the pastry. Bake for 45–50 minutes until the pastry is golden brown on top. If it is beginning to burn cover with foil. The filo/phyllo pastry will curl up once baked. However, some people sprinkle water onto their baklava prior to baking to prevent the fillo/phyllo from curling up, so you can do it this way if you prefer.

Immediately, while still hot, pour the cold syrup over the baklava, ensuring it seeps into every crevice. Leave to cool completely before serving. Do not cover or refrigerate as the fillo/phyllo will become soggy. When ready to serve, chop the remaining 1 tablespoon of pistachio nuts and sprinkle over the top.

200 g/1¹/₃ cups shelled unsalted pistachios, plus 1 tablespoon extra to serve

100 g/²/₃ cup each of whole almonds and pecan nuts

150 g/³/₄ cup coconut palm sugar

a good pinch of sea salt

¹/₂ teaspoon ground cinnamon

¹/₄ teaspoon ground cardamom

5 tablespoons coconut butter or oil, melted

20 filo/phyllo sheets, cut into 15 x 25-cm/6 x 12-in. rectangles

SYRUP

180 ml/³/₄ cup pure maple syrup

120 ml/¹/₂ cup water

1 cinnamon stick

freshly squeezed juice of ¹/₂ orange

freshly squeezed juice and zest of ¹/₂ lemon

2 cardamom pods, bashed open

a 15 x 25 cm/6 x 10 in. cake pan, lined with parchment paper

SERVES 12

Blood orange granita

Blood oranges, so called because of the deep red colour of their flesh and juice, are particularly associated with Sicily and add authenticity to this classic Sicilian dessert.

400 ml/1³/₄ cups spring water
200 g/1 cup caster/superfine sugar
600 ml/2¹/₂ cups freshly squeezed blood orange juice (about 15 oranges)

an ice cream maker

SERVES 4

In a saucepan set over medium heat, gently heat the spring water until it reaches boiling point. Remove from the heat and stir in the sugar until it dissolves. Let the syrup cool for 30 minutes.

Pass the blood orange juice through a sieve/strainer to remove any pips or bits of flesh.

When the syrup has cooled, add the blood orange juice and stir briefly to mix. Pour into the ice cream maker and churn freeze according to the manufacturer's instructions.

When it is ready, transfer the mixture to a shallow container. Return to the freezer for 1 hour to firm up. Remove from the

freezer and use a fork to scrape the surface of the ice to produce coarse granules. You can also do this straight from the ice cream maker for a softer finish.

Spoon the granules into glasses or bowls and serve immediately.

Cantaloupe melon sorbet

The cantaloupe melon has a special link with Italy, named as it is after the commune Cantolupo near Tivoli, where the Pope used to spend his summers. It is sweet and juicy and perfect for sorbets.

In a saucepan set over medium heat, gently heat 160 ml/⅔ cup of the spring water until it reaches boiling point. Remove from the heat, add the lemon juice and stir in 150 g/¾ cup of the sugar until it dissolves. Leave the syrup to cool for 30 minutes.

Put the melon and the remaining water and sugar in a food processor and blitz to a purée. Add the cooled syrup and the remaining lemon juice and blend briefly again until thoroughly mixed.

Pour the mixture into the ice cream maker and churn freeze according to the manufacturer's instructions.

The sorbet is best served immediately or can be kept in the freezer for up to 3–4 days.

310 ml/1⅓ cups spring water
freshly squeezed juice of ½ lemon
210 g/1 cup caster/superfine sugar
400 g/14 oz. cantaloupe melon peeled, deseeded and chopped (about ½ melon)

an ice cream maker

SERVES 4

Sorrento lemon sorbet

Sorrento is famous for its lemons, which are huge and weigh down the boughs of the trees on the roadside along the beautiful Amalfi coast. Reserve the husks and serve the lemon sorbet inside them in the traditional way.

610 ml/2½ cups spring water
200 ml/¾ cup freshly squeezed lemon juice (about 5 lemons), husks reserved
240 g/1 cup plus 3 tablespoons caster/superfine sugar

an ice cream maker

SERVES 4

In a saucepan set over medium heat, gently heat 160 ml/⅔ cup of the spring water until it reaches boiling point. Remove from the heat, add 2 tablespoons of the lemon juice and stir in 160 g/¾ cup of the sugar until it dissolves. Leave the syrup to cool for 30 minutes.

Put the remaining lemon juice, water and sugar in a jug/pitcher and whisk together. Add the cooled syrup and whisk briefly again until thoroughly mixed.

Pour the mixture into the ice cream maker and churn freeze according to the manufacturer's instructions.

Serve the sorbet spooned into the reserved lemon husks.

Sorbet is best served immediately but can be kept in the freezer for up to 3–4 days.

Tiramisú gelato

What could be better than real Italian gelato combined with another of Italy's most famous sweet exports? Tiramisú literally means 'lift me up' in Italian, which this delicious, creamy gelato is guaranteed to do!

600 ml/2 cups whole milk

150 ml/²/₃ cup whipping/heavy cream

50 ml/3 tablespoons port wine

3 egg yolks, plus 1 egg white

1 vanilla pod/bean, split lengthways

150 g/³/₄ cup caster/superfine sugar

200 ml/³/₄ cup prepared espresso coffee, chilled

5 Savoiardi (ladyfinger) biscuits/cookies, broken into small pieces

chocolate curls, to garnish

an ice cream maker

SERVES 4

Put the milk and cream in a small saucepan and heat gently until it reaches boiling point. Add the port wine and the egg yolks and whisk together. Add the vanilla pod/bean, pour the mixture into a heat-resistant bowl and refrigerate for 20 minutes.

In a large mixing bowl and using an electric hand whisk, beat together the sugar and egg white until it forms soft peaks when the beaters are lifted out of the mixture. Add 150 ml/²/₃ cup of the coffee and quickly whisk in.

Remove the chilled milk mixture from the refrigerator and discard the vanilla pod/bean. Pour into the sugar and egg mixture and whisk for a further 20 seconds.

Pour the mixture into the ice cream maker and churn freeze according to the manufacturer's instructions.

While the mixture is freezing, dip the Savoiardi biscuits/cookies into the remaining coffee. About 5 minutes before the end of the process, add the soaked biscuits/cookies into the mixture in the ice cream maker, and continue churning so they are mixed through.

The gelato is best served immediately or can be kept in the freezer for up to 3–4 days. Serve garnished with chocolate curls.

Almond affogato

Affogato, meaning 'drowned', is a classic Italian way to serve gelato. Drown scoops of gelato with a shot of hot espresso. Almond and coffee is a perfect combination, but you could try it with other gelato flavours such as Madagascan Vanilla, Bacio or Hazelnut. This recipe makes enough gelato for eight servings, but if fewer servings are required, simply store the remaining gelato in the freezer to enjoy another time.

500 ml/2 cups whole milk

165 ml/²/₃ cup whipping/heavy cream

140 g/1 cup shelled almonds

¹/₂ teaspoon sea salt

165 g/³/₄ cup caster/superfine sugar

1 egg white

shots espresso made with organic 100% Arabica beans, to serve

an ice cream maker

SERVES 8

Put the milk and cream in a small saucepan and heat gently until it reaches boiling point. Pour the mixture into a heat-resistant bowl and refrigerate for 20 minutes.

In a dry frying pan/skillet, lightly toast the almonds with the salt and set aside to cool. When cooled, grind the almonds to a paste in a food processor.

In a large mixing bowl and using an electric hand whisk, beat together the sugar and egg white until it forms soft peaks when the beaters are lifted out of the mixture. Stir in the almond paste, add the chilled milk mixture and whisk for a further 20 seconds.

Pour the mixture into the gelato maker and churn freeze according to the manufacturer's instructions.

Prepare shots of espresso using an espresso machine or an Italian moka. Place a scoop of the gelato into each coffee cup and serve with a shot of espresso on the side so guests can pour the hot coffee over the gelato and enjoy immediately.

Apricot and orange gelato

Gelato must be one of Italy's most loved and appreciated exports. This version uses apricot and orange. For a change, serve it between crisp wafers, biscuits/cookies or even slices of brioche, a traditional idea.

Put the chopped apricots in a saucepan and cover with boiling water by about 3 cm/1 in. Return to the boil, reduce the heat and simmer for 10 minutes. Turn off the heat. Leave to stand for 5 minutes.

Put the apricots and their cooking water in a blender (for smooth texture) or food processor (for coarse texture), then add the sugar, orange zest, orange and lemon juices, orange flower water and liqueur. Blend well. Add the mascarpone pieces. Blend briefly until the mixture is even and smooth. Pour out half and set aside.

Add the cream to the machine. Blend very briefly again until incorporated, then pour both mixtures into a large bowl, stirring well. Cool, if necessary, over iced water.

Transfer the mixture to an ice cream maker and churn for 20–35 minutes or until thick. Spoon into a freezerproof container, cover and freeze until time to use. Alternatively, freeze in the container, covered, for 6 hours, beating it once, after 3 hours. Serve in scoops or slices with biscuits or cake, if using.

Note

When sharply flavoured fresh apricots are in season, halve, pit and grill or bake 500 g/1 lb. (8–12 fruit) until they are collapsed, golden and tender. Use these in place of the dried apricots: they need no further cooking.

250 g/1¼ cups dried apricots, chopped

175 g/¾ cup plus 2 tablespoons caster/ superfine sugar

2 teaspoons freshly grated orange zest and 250 ml/1 cup freshly squeezed orange juice, about 2–3 oranges

3 tablespoons freshly squeezed lemon juice, about 1 medium lemon

1 teaspoon orange flower water

2 tablespoon Cointreau (or other citrus liqueur)

250 g/8 oz. mascarpone cheese, in pieces

400 ml/1¾ cups single/light cream

8–12 wafers, biscuits/cookies, sliced brioche or lemon cakes (optional)

an ice cream maker

1.5-l/6-cup freezerproof container with a lid

SERVES 4–6

Prosecco cocktails

Perhaps the most famous of all Venetian cocktails, the Bellini was invented by Giuseppe Cipriani at the celebrated Harry's Bar in Venice around 70 years ago. It's a mixture of fresh white peach juice and Prosecco. To stay true to the original flavour (and enjoy the best cocktail), only white peaches (not yellow) will do. And absolutely no canned peaches! Please!

CLASSIC

40 ml/3 tablespoons freshly made white peach purée
480 ml/2 cups Prosecco

MAKES 4

Pour the peach purée into chilled Champagne flutes. Pour in the Prosecco and stir gently.

Serve immediately.

STRAWBERRY AND BASIL

5 ripe strawberries
1 teaspoon white sugar
a small handful of fresh basil leaves
120 ml/½ cup Prosecco

MAKES 1

Whizz the strawberries and sugar together in a blender to make a purée. Pour the purée into a jug/pitcher, add a little of the Prosecco and the basil. Bash with a blunt object until lots of flavour has been released. Pour the mixture through a strainer into a chilled glass. Pour over the remaining Prosecco and stir gently. Serve immediately.

PEAR

200 ml/¾ cup pear purée
480 ml/2 cups Prosecco

MAKES 4

Pour the pear purée into chilled glasses. Pour in the Prosecco and stir gently. Serve immediately.

Limoncello

Delicious and wickedly refreshing. Many trattorias make their own – and when it runs out, you have to wait a long time for the new batch. It is best kept in the freezer and poured into frozen glasses. It is made wherever lemons are grown, especially the Amalfi coast.

2 large lemons, plus the freshly squeezed juice of 1 lemon

475 ml/2 cups pure spirits/liquor, such as vodka or grappa

375 g/1¾ cups sugar

a preserving jar, at least 500 ml/1 pint
sterilized bottles (see page 4),
750 ml /3 cups total

MAKES ABOUT 750 ML/3 CUPS

Wash and scrub the lemons in warm soapy water. Rinse and dry. Carefully peel the zest from the lemons in long strips and put in a large preserving jar. Pour in the alcohol, seal tightly and leave in a dark place for 2 months.

After 2 months, put the sugar in a saucepan with 250 ml/1 cup water and the strained juice of 1 lemon. Heat gently until the sugar dissolves. Cool. Open the preserving jar with the lemon-flavoured spirits and pour in the sugar syrup. Stir well, and let stand for 2–3 hours. Strain through a fine sieve/strainer or coffee paper and pour into sterilized bottles. Seal and leave in a cool dark place for 1 week. Store in the freezer, where it will thicken but not freeze.

Negroni

Though an aperitivo, not a digestivo, this is the best cocktail, in or out of Italy. It was invented by a Florentine nobleman, Camillo Negroni. He added a drop of gin to his favourite cocktail, the Americano (Campari, red vermouth and soda), for extra kick.

30 ml/1 oz. gin

30 ml/1 oz. Campari

20 ml/¾ oz. sweet (red) vermouth

a wide twist of orange zest

a cocktail shaker

SERVES 1

Put the gin, Campari and vermouth in an ice-filled cocktail shaker. Shake until well chilled and strain into a chilled cocktail glass.

Cut a piece of orange zest about 2 x 4 cm/1 x 2 in. There must be no white pith attached – this will stop the oil being released from the zest. Holding the orange zest in one hand, hold a lit match over the glass with the other. Hold the orange zest about 2 cm/1 in. above the flame and squeeze the zest quickly. When done correctly, a burst of flame will come from the oils being released from the orange zest, leaving their aroma and adding a note of burnt orange to the cocktail. Drop the twist into the drink and serve immediately.

Index

Photography credits

KEY *ph = photographer a = above;*
b = below; r = right; l = left; i = insert.

Food

Jan Baldwin *Pages 31bg, 74, 75, 124bg*

Steve Baxter *Page 30r*

Martin Brigdale *Pages 4r, 6ar, 7, 14l, 15r, 16r, 17r, 31i, 33, 60, 66l, 73a, 82, 83, 106i, 118, 132l, 140l, 144, 148, 149, 154, 156, 163r, 164, 171l, 173*

Earl Carter *Pages 102r, 111r*

Peter Cassidy *Pages 3, 4l, 6ba and al, 15l, 20, 36, 40–44, 50, 51l, 57, 58, 66r, 70r, 72–73b, 76r, 78, 79, 80a, 87i, 88i, 89r, 90, 91, 96br, 108a, 109b, 116r, 125, 127, 129, 132r, 136r, 143, 150, 151bg, 160l, 163l, 169b, 171r*

Jean Cazals *Pages 155r, 157b, 158i*

Tara Fisher *Pages 138, 166*

Jonathan Gregson *Page 55r*

Richard Jung *Pages 107l and bg, 108b, 109a, 112–114, 116l, 117*

Mowie Kay *Page 172*

Erin Kunkel *Pages 97–99, 139, 157a, 159*

William Lingwood *Pages 55l, 165*

Paul Massey *Page 22r*

David Munns *Pages 27–29, 46, 64, 76l, 104, 147r, 155l*

Steve Painter *Pages 2, 11, 18, 19l, 22l, 23, 25, 26, 32, 45, 47, 54, 63, 67, 68, 71, 77, 80b, 81, 93, 94, 102l, 103, 110, 115, 122, 127, 133, 136l, 145, 146b, 158bg, 167b, 168, 169a, 170*

William Reavell *Page 106bg*

Mark Scott *Page 16l*

Georgia Glynn-Smith *Pages 38, 96l and a*

Debi Treloar *Pages 10, 14r, 30l, 70l, 137, 147l, 160r, 167a*

Kate Whitaker *Pages 5, 8, 12, 52, 59, 61, 85–87bg, 123, 124i, 130, 131, 146a*

Clare Winfield *Pages 1, 19r, 21, 39l, 48r, 51r, 84, 88bg, 89l, 121, 134, 135, 140r, 141, 152, 161*

Interiors

17, 48l and 126 Vanni and Nicoletta Calamai's home near Siena. **Ph Chris Tubbs** 34 www.les-sardines.com. **Ph Claire Richardson** 39r A house in Maremma, Tuscany designed by Contemporanea. **Ph Chris Tubbs** 53 The home in Denmark of Charlotte Lynggaard, designer of Ole Lynggaard Copenhagen. **Ph Christopher Drake** 107r Toia Saibene and Giuliana Magnifico's home in Lucignano, Tuscany. **Ph Chris Tubbs** 111l Hôtel Le Sénéchal, Ars en Ré, designed by Christophe Ducharme Architecte. **Ph Paul Massey** 128 ph Andrew Wood and Rick Haylor 151i Giorgio and Ilaria Miani's Podere Casellacce in Val d'Orcia. **Ph Chris Tubbs** Endpapers Marina Ferrara Pignatelli's home in Val d'Orcia, Tuscany. **Ph Chris Tubbs**

Recipe credits

Valerie Aikman-Smith
Chocolate cakes with Armagnac prunes; Gazpacho with smoked salted croutons; Grilled lobster with chive blossom butter; Lemon & pepper ricotta gnocchi; Mint & lemon thyme lamb skewers; Pissaladiere pizza with Provençal olive relish; Rack of lamb with harissa & pomegranate

Miranda Ballard
Asparagus & prosciutto gratin; Bresaola, oven tomato & buffalo mozzarella salad; Caramelized red onion & salami pizza; Chorizo & bean burger; Goat's cheese & salami frittata; Mediterranean pasta bake; Mortadella, olive tapenade & rocket sandwich; Paella; Pancake calzones; Parma ham & melon; Proscuitto, artichoke, fig & Roquefort salad; Puttanesca relish & olive tapenade; Spanish charcuterie board; Warm infused olives

Ghillie Basan
Aubergines stuffed with onions & tomatoes; Chargrilled prawns; Chargrilled sardine wrapped in vine leaves with tomatoes; Cumin lamb kebabs with hot hummus; Lamb & porcini kebabs with sage & parmesan; Lemon chicken kebabs wrapped in aubergine; Roasted baby peppers stuffed with feta; Stuffed & chargrilled sardines; Summer vegetable kebabs with pesto; Swordfish kebabs with orange & sumac; Vine wrapped white fish kebabs with tangy herb sauce

Jordan Bourke
Ajo blanco with melon; Baklava; Gnocchi with tomato, parsley & almonds; Pan fried langoustines with salsa agresto

Maxine Clark
Amaretti with pine nuts; Barbecued devilled grilled chicken; Fluffy ricotta fritters; Grilled mixed vegetable salad with balsamic dressing; Grilled tuna steaks with peperonata; Limoncelllo; Marinated fresh anchovies; Negroni; Polenta with sausage ragu; Potato pizza; Risotto with red wine, mushrooms & pancetta; Stewed fennel with olive, lemon & chilli; Strawberries with balsamic syrup & mascarpone ice cream; Three marinated antipasti; Tomato mozzarella & basil salad; Tuscan bean soup; Warm zabaglione pears poached in marsala wine

Clare Ferguson
Apricot and orange gelato; Catalan chickpea salad; Chorizo in red wine; Fougasse; French lemon tart; Greek cheese savoury; Grilled asparagus with prosciutto; Italian bean dip; Panna cotta with rose petal syrup; Pasta alla genovese; Provençal beef daube with lemon & parsley; Sicilian tuna; Souvlaki pitta; Spanish clams with ham; Spanish duck with olives; Spanish flans; Spanish potato omelette; Spanish tart with peppers; Stuffed aubergines

Ursula Ferrigno
Chocolate and cherry amaretti; Falsomagro beef & pork; Fried courgette flowers; Fried vegetables with tomato sauce; Grilled herb pork skewers; Red peppers stuffed with fennel; Sicilian potato croquettes; Tuna carpaccio with lemon parsley sauce

Tori Finch
Lemon, garlic & chilli potato salad; Rosemary skewered sausages

Amy Ruth Finegold
Spelt and spinach salad with pear & prosciutto; Wild rice salad with artichokes, peaches & pine nuts

Mat Follas
Artichoke with garlic butter; Barbecued mackerel with tomato & onion; BBQ octopus with grilled lemons; Bouillabaisse; Goat's cheese & marjoram ravioli marinara; Grilled tuna niçoise salad; Monkfish & harissa kebabs; Mussels three ways; Panzanella-stuffed tomatoes; Ricotta tarts with pea & mint; Sardine crostini; Savoy cabbage ratatouille parcels; Spelt-stuffed squid; Tempura squid; Tuna & anchovy pizza; Whitebait fritters

Liz Franklin
Prosecco cocktails

Acland Geddes & Pedro da Silva
Bruschetta of caponata & marinated mozzarella; Gorgonzola & honey; Grilled squid with chorizo, feta & asparagus salad; Mussel, cannellini & pancetta soup with rosemary oil; Osso buco with orange gremolata; Roasted figs with Parma ham; Saffron aioli & hazelnut picada; Tuna & melon tartare with paprika crisps

Jenny Linford
Black garlic tricolore salad; Broad bean, feta & dill salad; Cherry tomato bruschetta; Crab and basil linguine; Fattoush; Fig, honey & ricotta cheesecake; Greek style baked fish with tomatoes; Griddled tuna with bean purée & gremolata; Grilled mussels with wild garlic crumb; Grilled trout fillets with sauce vierge; Harissa sardines with tomato salad; Lamb steaks with cherry tomato & anchovy sauce; Mediterranean garlicky fish stew; Orange syrup semolina cake; Panzanella; Pappa al pomodoro; Patatas bravas; Polenta puttanesca; Provençal stuffed tomatoes; Risotto nero with garlic prawns; Roast garlic & rosemary focaccia; Spaghetti alle vongole; Spaghetti con aglio, olio e pepperoncino; Spanish garlic soup; Spanish prawns; Sun-blush orange, tomato & burrata salad; Tabbouleh; Tomato & fennel salad; Tomato, freekeh & avocado salad; Tomato, melon & feta salad; Tomato parmesan frittata; Tomato tart; Wild garlic pasta primavera

Adriano di Petrillo
Almond affogato; Blood orange granita; Melon sorbet; Sorrento lemon sorbet; Tiramisu gelato

Annie Rigg
Arancini

Shelagh Ryan
Caponata with grilled polenta & whipped feta; Mushroom stew with walnut gremolata on soft polenta; Orzo with roast courgettes & tomato dressing; Sautéed mixed mushrooms with lemon & herb feta; Tomato soup with fennel, garlic & basil drizzle

Laura Washburn
Honey parfait with meringue and pistachios